RECLAIMING FREEDOM:

Modern Threats to Speech & Religion

RECLAIMING FREEDOM:

Modern Threats to Speech & Religion

Proceedings of the
Christopher Dawson Centre Colloquium 2022

edited by David Daintree

Christopher Dawson Press
Hobart, Tasmania, Australia
2023

The Christopher Dawson Centre for Cultural Studies
35 Tower Road
New Town
Tasmania 7008
Australia

www.dawsoncentre.org

Copyright © David Daintree 2023

ALL RIGHTS RESERVED. This book contains material protected under International and Federal Copyright Laws and Treaties. Any unauthorised reprint or use of this material is prohibited. No part of this book may be reproduced or transmitted in any form or by any means, electronic or mechanical, including photocopying, recording, or by any information storage and retrieval system without express written permission from the publisher.

ISBN: 9780645599305 (print)

ACKNOWLEDGEMENTS

Layout by Eilidh Direen

Cover design by Veronika Winkels

Cover image: *Madonna col Bambino, Santa Apollonia, San Bernardino e quattro angeli, tempera su tavola* by Sano di Pietro. Museo d'Arte Sacra della Val d'Arbia, before 1481.

Contents

7   **David Daintree**
Introduction

11   **David Collits**
Truth, Gnosis and Freedom

33   **Kenneth Crowther**
Free Speech as 'Ouroboros': Self-Devouring Freedoms

51   **Kevin Donnelly**
Repressive Tolerance: Enforcing Mind Control

61   **Monica Doumit**
How Safe are Religious Exemptions?

78   **Lucas Mclennan**
Christianity and Free Expression: An Uneasy Relationship

93   **Archbishop Julian Porteous**
The Two Wings – Faith and Reason

101   **Lyle Shelton**
Picking Up the Tools of Democracy

112   **Alex Sidhu**
Freedom of Speech and Religion: The Christian Difference

132   **David Van Gend**
'Citizens of No Mean City'

148   **Veronika Winkels**
Shepherding Wolves to Save our Freedoms

161   **Our Contributors**

INTRODUCTION
David Daintree

THE CHRISTOPHER DAWSON Centre for Cultural Studies, founded in 2013 by Archbishop Julian Porteous of Hobart, was given the task of 'advancing the good name of the Catholic intellectual tradition'. It was made clear that it was to operate at arm's length from the Church and enjoy a high degree of independence, for its brief was not so much to proclaim the Gospel as to demonstrate its *reasonableness*. As Christians we in the Dawson Centre insist that there is no conflict between faith and reason, but our focus is on the intellect alone, leaving the preaching of the Gospel to others commissioned and better gifted than ourselves to teach it. We maintain that to believe the Gospel is not a naive or feeble superstition, but an intelligent act of faith, firmly founded on reason, history, anthropology, human experience and that natural law written in our hearts,[1] according to Christian belief, whose existence was recognised even by the pagans:

> *There exists one true law, one right reckoning in accord with nature. It is common to all men, unchanging, everlasting. Its commandments call us to duty and its prohibitions deter us*

---

[1] *Epistle to the Romans* ii.14-16

from deceit ... Established by divine authority this law may not be annulled, nor abrogated wholly or in any part. Neither government nor people can absolve us from obedience to it.[1]

The Dawson Centre's chief purpose, then, is to host and promote discussion on the place of human 'reckoning' or Reason in the formation of Faith. Though we are based in Hobart (which we sometimes cheekily describe as *The Athens of the South*!) we have a world-wide following. The internet enables us to challenge the tyranny of distance, our talks are uploaded to the web, and our annual Colloquium attracts speakers from further afield. When we speak of the *Catholic Intellectual Tradition* we take a broad view, living as we do at a time when Christians of all denominations are closing ranks against an often hostile world and appreciating each other's grand traditions. We honour the great Protestant intellectual achievements and are proud and delighted to have Christians of the reformed tradition on our committee. Moreover we have followers who are not believers yet recognise the central part that Christianity has played in the emergence of Western Civilisation.

The focus of the 2022 Colloquium was on freedom of speech. All the papers presented at that event are gathered together in this volume. As editor I decided to arrange the papers in alphabetical order of the authors' names, admitting no other hierarchy of precedence, for all are of a very high standard and all contribute in one way or another to our understanding of the issues—legal, political, historical or theological.

1   Est quidem vera lex, recta ratio, naturæ congruens, diffusa in omnes, constans, sempiterna, quae vocet ad officium jubendo, vetando a fraude deterreat ... huic legi nec abrogari fas est, neque derogari ex hac aliquid licet, neque tota abrogari potest; nec vero aut per senatum, aut per populum solvi hac lege possumus. (Cicero, *de re publica* iii.33)

INTRODUCTION

'Freedom of speech' is one of those glib notions that almost everyone claims to believe in, but few understand or even, in practice, tolerate. Much is said and written today about restrictions to that freedom being imposed upon religious people, particularly, and most if not all the writers in this book hold the view that this is or ought to be a serious concern. But this is a dilemma, for one man's freedom is another's restraint. There never has been a time in history when all people enjoyed absolute freedom to say what they think, nor could there be: there is always a need for compromise, and in every age there have been strong and sometimes severe restrictions on free expression.

There was never a golden age. Christians have suffered persecution for their beliefs, but so have non-Christians, often at our hands. Throughout the course of the past 200 years the scope of free speech has been widened, at least in western nations, to such an extent that it is usually now thought of as some kind of 'right'. This movement towards free expression reached its zenith in the 60s of the last century when almost all forms of censorship were abandoned, universities and even schools shied away from exercising any kind of moral authority over their students, pornography flourished in ever more disgusting ways, and self-indulgence became for most of us the only moral imperative.

Today the pendulum is moving in the other direction, though not always in ways of which we approve. 'Wokery' is a new and godless manifestation of puritanism. The so-called *Woke*, the Politically Correct, are deeply intolerant of opinions that do not fit the prevailing liberal narrative. Hypocrisy has found novel and breathtakingly dreadful ways of making life difficult for ordinary people. We are all against bullying, but there seem to be more bullies than ever out there telling us what to think, what to eat, what to do with our leisure, what words to use and not to use. Words even change their meaning:

marriage, *male*, *female* no longer mean what they used to mean. The traditional mainstream media are willing participants in this process: commentary seems to be taking the place of reporting, and the news we are offered has been pre-selected and interpreted for our supposed edification, not so much for the truth of its content (after all, what is truth?) but for our correction. Views that do not conform to the accepted line are either not reported at all, or else quite viciously and often ignorantly condemned. On matters such as the response to Covid, gender fluidity, renewable energy, abortion, euthanasia, white complicity in the ills of the world, there is only one position that is acceptable, and divergence is treated with scorn. Anyone who has been banned by Face Book, or who has tried to find on the internet alternatives to modern secular orthodoxy, knows that this is the case.

Many of our writers have suffered abuse or discrimination because of the non-conforming views they hold. Some have been prosecuted. Some have had their livelihoods threatened. Most have felt constrained in one way or another and unable to express openly their beliefs on matters of great weight. We are also aware that the gulf between the wokery of the so-called intellectuals who try to form public opinion and ordinary people is widening to breaking point. The essays in this book are important because they show us that we are not alone: we have friends and allies who are intelligent and eloquent, and the ground is shifting at last. There will be no certain victory in this world, but the game is worth the candle, and we should enjoy the adventure:

'*For there is good news yet to hear and fine things to be seen, Before we go to Paradise by way of Kensal Green.*'

TRUTH, GNOSIS AND FREEDOM[1]
David Collits

ABSTRACT

Contemporary Australian culture exerts tremendous implicit and explicit control over the speech and therefore life and thought of its members. A general aggression towards the public claims of religion about God, creation, humanity and sex reflect a suspicion of 'unorthodox' speech, which does not conform to prevailing ideologies, as well as a more fundamental suspicion or devaluing of truth. The relationship between the freedoms of speech and religion bears consequently examination. Freedom of communication is not absolute. Its end is not to permit communication for the sake of it, but to enable individuals to pursue and discover truth. Inevitably, then, freedom of expression is tied to freedom of religion. A healthy society gives genuine religion room in its worship, preaching and interventions in the public square to propose absolute truth claims, to allow seekers of truth the capacity to discover it. A deeply unhealthy society will exclude such communication, as well robust

1   Dr David Collits, Lecturer in Catholic Theology at the University of Notre Dame, Sydney Campus, Australia. The views expressed herein are of course the author's own and only the author's.

discussions about what are ultimately prudential judgments. At the heart of culture is theology (or a-theology). This paper proposes a theological solution, therefore, as being at the heart of any genuine attempt to reach a practical solution to the threats posed to freedom of speech and religion.

ENTRÉE

It is A.D. 1349 in the remotest north of Norway. The nuns of Rein Convent have so far escaped the Black Plague that has spread across Europe. Alas, however, the deadliest pandemic in human history – some estimates suggest up to 25 million Europeans died, including one-third of Englishmen – soon spread into Scandinavia.¹ 'Death and horror and suffering seemed to push people into a world without time'.² Nuns begin to succumb. The locals are in the grip of panic, ready to embrace any technique to alleviate the pandemic. Rumours reach the nuns that some locals, not entirely free of pagan superstition, have kidnapped a small boy, Tore, the son of an outcast woman, Steinunn, at the margins of society. Their design is to sacrifice the child that night in the local cemetery to propitiate the goddess of death or plague giantess, Hel (for Marvel fans, Hel was the child of Loki, Thor's duplicitous brother).

One of the nuns, sensing the spiritual danger to the men and the physical danger to the child, encourages her sisters in religion to intervene: 'We can't just sit here while Christian souls sell themselves to the Devil right on our doorstep'.³ And so they '[step] out into the raw, cold winter night', Christ-like into the darkness of death in order to save the child's life and

---

1   'Black Death' in *A Dictionary of World History*, 2ⁿᵈ ed. (Oxford: Oxford University Press, 2006), p. 74.
2   Sigrid Undset, *Kristin Lavransdatter*, trans. Tiina Nunnally (London: Penguin Books, 2005), p. 1104.
3   Ibid., p. 1109.

the men from themselves. They reach them just in time: the men were beginning to shovel dirt onto the child, who was sitting in an open grave. The nun tells them to 'Go home and thank God that you were saved before you committed an act you might never be able to atone for'.[1] The locals, however, are too fearful of the plague yet to step aside. One, Arntor, becomes aggressive and threatening, and asks, 'Isn't it better to sacrifice *one* than for all of us to perish?'[2] To which the nun responds: 'The worst thing, for both *us* and for *you*, would have been if we had stayed home while you went about building your home in the hottest Hell'.[3] In the end, Arntor will only back down if the nun 'puts her money where her mouth is' and backs-up her declamation with action. Accordingly, the nun willingly seeks out the boy's mother, who had died and whose remains had been left in a remote hut, to retrieve the body and give it Christian burial. She does so, catches the plague and dies but Tore survives and the locals are prevented from engaging in child sacrifice.

CLAIM

The concern of this paper is: to unearth, with the help of Eric Voegelin and Joseph Ratzinger/Pope Benedict XVI, the epistemological foundations of present threats to freedom of religion and freedom of speech by a creeping totalitarianism; and to propose some theological and practical starting points in response. The claim of the paper is that Voegelin and Ratzinger's analysis of gnosis makes intelligible today's phenomenon of restricted speech and that this analysis shows the importance of the search for transcendence and welcome being given to revelation in overcoming those threats.

1   Ibid., p. 1111.
2   Ibid., p. 1111 (emphasis added).
3   Ibid., p. 1112 (emphasis added).

CONTEXT: CREEPING TOTALITARIANISM

In his Gifford Lectures of 1948-1949, Christopher Dawson observed that:

> It would be a strange fatality if the great revolution by which Western man has subdued nature to his purposes should end in the loss of his own spiritual freedom, but this might well happen if an increasing technical control of the state over the life and thought of its members should coincide with a qualitative decline in the standards of our culture.[1]

In many ways, it is submitted, we have succumbed to the loss of spiritual freedom Dawson anticipated, not least in the loss of the standards of our culture, particularly the desire to pursue truth in charity (c.f. Eph 4:15). This fatality flows from contemporary culture's replacement of God with a gnostic 'civilisation'. 'Civilisation' in this context can be understood as attempts to progress society towards a liberal-Marxist utopia, according to an immanently progressive logic.[2] That utopia wishes for all constraints on human will, whether moral, biological, sexual, marital, familial, national or religious, to be removed, and the absence of constraint to be safeguarded by the ever-expanding state.[3]

---

1 Christopher Dawson, *Religion and the Rise of Western Culture* (New York: Doubleday, 1991), p. 14.

2 For Ratzinger, both Marxism and liberalism 'are ultimately shaped by the idea of progress, which, of course, connects with a strange eschatological consciousness: Finally, at some point in the dialectic of human history, society's perfected state will inevitably arise …' Joseph Ratzinger, Johann Baptist Metz, Jürgen Moltmann, Eveline Goodman-Thau, *The End of Time? The Provocation of Talking about God*, edited and translated by J Matthew Ashley (New York/Mahwah, NJ: Paulist Press, 2004), p. 14.

3 See Patrick Deneen, *Why Liberalism Failed* (New Haven and London: Yale University Press, 2018), pp. 46-47. A clear articulation of the modern faith in the realization of the will is found in the US

The totalising tendencies of the contemporary state threaten the spiritual core that is at the heart of Western civilisation and its championing of religion and the liberty of the Spirit ordered to truth, beauty and goodness.[1] Twentieth century German-American Eric Voegelin, shortly after Dawson delivered his cultural diagnosis, stated that the 'death of the spirit is the price of progress'.[2] The sacrifice of spiritual life and values is an inevitable concomitant of civilizational progress. This is so because the civilizational system replaces God as the object of religious yearning and loyalty, and, in so doing, absolutizes civilisation.

Voegelin makes this comment in his analysis of what Ratzinger identifies as the 'secularization of Christian eschatological thought', the strain of modern philosophical and political thought and action that seeks and attempts to effect redemption within an immanent temporal frame.[3] Voegelin describes the phenomenon as constituted by 'human energies [being] thrown into the great enterprise of salvation through world-immanent action'.[4] The energies of hope in redemption are directed away from prayerful expectation of the Parousia

---

1992 Supreme Court decision of *Planned Parenthood v Casey* 505 US 833 (1992) at p. 851: 'At the heart of liberty is the right to define one's own concept of existence, of meaning, of the universe, and of the mystery of human life.' Happily, this decision was overturned in *Dodds v Jackson Women's Health Organization* 597 US __ (2022).

[1] C.f. Jean-Pierre Torrell, *Saint Thomas Aquinas, vol 2: Spiritual Master*, trans. Robert Royal (Washington DC: Catholic University of America Press, 2003), p. 172.

[2] Eric Voegelin, *The New Science of Politics: An Introduction* (Chicago and London: The University of Chicago Press, 1987), p. 131.

[3] Joseph Ratzinger, *Eschatology: Death and Eternal Life*, 2nd edition, trans. Michael Waldstein, trans. edited by Aidan Nichols (Washington DC: Catholic University of America Press, 1988), p. 13.

[4] Voegelin, *New Science of Politics*, p. 131.

into human-led action directed to the definitive realization of salvation *within history*'.[1]

Voegelin's singular contribution to the identification and description of the phenomenon of the 'immanentization of the Christian eschaton' was to identify it as a form of gnosis.[2] In brief terms, an ancient Christian heresy, Gnosticism broadly claims that salvation is based on the possession of exhaustive and comprehensive knowledge of the fullness of truth,

1 Joseph Ratzinger, *The God of Jesus Christ: Meditations on the Triune God*, 2nd ed., trans. Brian McNeil (San Francisco: Ignatius Press, 2008), p. 117 (emphasis added). Voegelin, along with thinkers such as Ratzinger and Karl Löwith, root the modern tendency to re-divinize society and to make history an idol in the thought of twelfth century Calabrian monk, Joachim of Flora (Fiore). Joachim's tri-partite periodization of history predicted a Third Age of the Spirit in which history would be transformed into the eschatological, 'intelligible state of perfection': Voegelin, *New Science of Politics*, pp. 107-132 (quotation on p. 118), Ratzinger, *Eschatology*, pp. 13, 211-213, Karl Löwith, *Meaning in History* (Chicago and London: The University of Chicago Press, 1949), pp. 145-159. Augustine's understanding of profane history as a *saeculum senescens*, an age that grows old awaiting its catastrophic transformation into the *eschaton*, is replaced by a view of secular history *itself and from within* tending towards its immanent perfection. Joachim laid the groundwork for Marx's Hegelian-dialectical view of the progression of history towards a proletariat utopia, in which the working class owns the means of production: Voegelin, pp. 118-121. Ratzinger highlights as another example, Hitler's Third Reich: Ratzinger, *God of Jesus Christ*, p. 117.

2 Voegelin, *New Science of Politics*, p. 121. Voegelin, of course, recognized that Gnosticism was one of several pathologies affecting modern civilization. He did not himself commit the intellectual sin of which he accused the Gnostics, that is, reducing everything to one particular explanatory theory: Eric Voegelin, *Science, Politics and Gnosticism: Two Essays by Eric Voegelin* (Wilmington, Delaware: ISI Books, 2004), p. xix.

a knowledge reserved to an elect (gnosis).[1] Modern gnosis particularly took the intellectual form of Hegel's idealism or Marx or Hitler's 'activist redemption of man and society'.[2] Gnosis, in this context, is the attempt to forestall the cognitive uncertainty characteristic of Christian faith, which says that the substance of what is hoped for is to be found in faith and faith alone (Heb 11:1). Gnosis is impatient with the apophaticism of Christianity and seeks to possess for itself a greater and total epistemic grasp of transcendence. It is the original sin of the human spirit's desire to know everything for itself without dependence on higher revelation.[3] It attempts, by natural reason alone, to create, in Josef Pieper's words, a 'total solution', which is an 'adequate reflection of the essential reality of the universe'.[4] Hence, Hegel's claim that 'The true form in which truth exists can only be the scientific system of truth'.[5] Human knowledge arrogates to itself the key of the knowledge of *all* things, transcendent and secular.

What in practice this means, however, is that the gnostic elite exclusively possesses what is considered acceptable knowledge. There can be no truth outside that which is knowable

1   John A Hardon, *Catholic Dictionary*, abridged and updated (New York: Image, 2013), p. 192.

2   Voegelin, *New Science of Politics*, pp. 123-124 (quotation on p. 124).

3   Compare the attitude of the Pslamist: 'O Lord, my heart is not lifted up, my eyes are not raised too high; I do not occupy myself with things too great and too marvelous for me' (Ps 1301:1 (RSVCE: Oxford/New York: Oxford University Press, 2004)).

4   Josef Pieper, *Guide to Thomas Aquinas*, trans. Richard and Clara Winston (San Francisco: Ignatius Press, 1991), p. 158, Voegelin, *New Science of Politics*, pp. 122-124, citing St Thomas Aquinas, *Summa Theologiae*, II-II, 4, 1.

5   Pieper, *Guide to Thomas Aquinas*, p. 158 quoting *Phänomenolgie des Geistes*, ed. J Hoffmesiter (Hamburg: Vorrede, 1952), p. 12.

according to the dictates of whichever gnostic movement is in power. An example is Friedrich Engels' epistemological claim that the successful results of 'experimental research and industry' disproved what he considered to be the fallacy that there cannot be an exhaustive knowledge of (material) reality. It is not accident that Engels' claim became part of the 'official doctrine of Bolshevism'.[1] That it is even possible to say that a political party or movement has an 'official doctrine' reveals both the secularisation of the eschaton and the monopolisation of truth in the hands of the 'Party', the priests of that religion.

Latent in the gnosis characteristic of progressive modernity is consequently totalitarianism, which is progressivism's endpoint. Voegelin observes that a civilisation, which has replaced God, will eventually meet its limit of progress, 'when an activist sect which represents the Gnostic truth organizes the civilization into an empire under its rule'.[2] He goes on: 'Totalitarianism, defined as the existential rule of Gnostic activists, is the end form of progressive civilisation'.[3] The trajectory of gnostic civilisation is totalitarianism, whether it is Soviet Russia or the creeping totalitarianism of contemporary liberal-Marxism.

---

1   Josef Pieper, *The Silence of St Thomas*, trans. John Murray SJ and Daniel O'Connor (South Bend, Indiana: St Augustine's Press, 1999), p. 92. It is well in this context to point out the scientism underlying connection between Hegel's claims of total scientific knowledge and the epistemology undergirding Marx's material dialecticism. Scientism, as Voegelin points out, is 'one of the strongest Gnostic movements in Western society', an observation as relevant in the 2020s as the 1950s: Voegelin, *New Science of Politics*, p. 127. Connecting Hegel to Marx is consequently the gnostic temptation to hold that all is knowable according to a scientific mode of knowledge, which in turn enables humanity to manipulate history according to its own immanently progressive logic.

2   Voegelin, *New Science of Politics*, p. 132.

3   Ibid.

TODAY'S GNOSIS AND THREATS TO HUMAN FREEDOM

Ratzinger acutely draws out the anthropological significance and dangers that gnosticism poses to wisdom, philosophical reflection and consequently, it can be added, to free political, economic and scientific inquiry. He observes that the Gnostics of the ancient period (the first Christian heretics) disdained philosophy as 'too little for them'.[1] Genuine philosophy is not acceptable to the gnostic mind because, in the words of Ratzinger, philosophy 'always remains a question and awaits an answer which it cannot give on its own'.[2] Gnosis does not tolerate the uncertainty inherent to philosophical speculation and its inherent openness to receiving from revelation the answers it cannot provide. In the words of Voegelin scholar Ellis Sandoz, Gnosticism is 'anti-philosophy', which does not love the being that precedes and conditions it. Rather, it 'desires dominion over being [so as] to *seize control over being*', which its intellectual system furthers.[3] As Ratzinger observes, gnosis 'pretend[s] to possess clear knowledge…in the sense of power to *master the world*'.[4] There is therefore a 'total claim of gnosis', which seeks to remove the uncertainty and therefore all questioning and ability to accept truth that is at the heart of what it means to be human.[5] The peculiarly modern and reductionist philosophies and movements of Hegelian historicism, 'positivism, Marxism, Freudianism, existentialism,

---

1   Joseph Ratzinger, *The Nature and Mission of Theology: Essays to Orient Theology in Today's Debates*, trans. Adrian Walker (San Francisco: Ignatius Press, 1995), p. 28.
2   Ibid., p. 28.
3   Ellis Sandoz, 'Intoduction' in Voegelin, *Science, Politics and Gnosticism*, p. xiii (emphasis added).
4   Ratzinger, *Nature and Mission of Theology*, p. 28 (emphasis added).
5   Ibid.

progressivism, utopianism, revolutionary activism, fascism, communism, national socialism' – all of which have residues in our culture – leads to the end of questioning as the distinctly philosophical pursuit of wisdom.[1]

So much of public discourse today is characterised precisely by such lack of fearless, questioning inquiry and willingness to receive and be informed by revealed truth. Contemporary Western culture, led by the state but aided and abetted by big business, the media and the academy, exerts tremendous implicit and explicit control over the speech and therefore life and thought of its members. The state itself has become an oversized actor in our lives. Alasdair MacIntyre observes: 'Let us then think of the contemporary state and the contemporary national economy as a huge, single, complex, heterogeneous, immensely powerful something or other.'[2] The 'immensely powerful something or other' has its fingers everywhere. Particularly apposite is Lord Sumption's observation that 'We have made a Leviathan of the state, expanding and harnessing its power in order to reduce the risks that threaten our well-being.'[3] Jeremy Bentham and Michel Foucault's Panopticon is an apt metaphor of how exposed we are to digital oversight, an example of the control exercised by the state-big business axis.

    1   Sandoz, op. cit., p. xiv.

    2   Alasdair MacIntyre, 'Toleration and the goods of conflict' in *Ethics and Politics, vol 2: Selected Essays* (Cambridge: Cambridge University Press, 2006), p. 211.

    3   Jonathan Sumption, *Trials of the State: Law and the Decline of Politics* (London: Profile Books, 2020), pp. 18-19. Elsewhere he writes that characteristic of modern law and bureaucratic regulation is 'its progressive invasion of the interstices of daily life': R *(on the application of Prudential plc and another) v Special Commissioner of Income Tax and another* [2013] UKSC 1 quoted in Dyson Heydon, *Selected Speeches and Papers*, ed. John Sackar and Thomas Prince (Sydney: The Federation Press, 2018), p. 181.

State and capitalist surveillance has the potential to monitor our every move and has already taken significant steps in that direction.[1]

A few examples will suffice of the imposition of various gnoses by these powerful actors and the intolerance of heterodox, particularly traditional Christian views, or simply different viewpoints. Does not the arcana of the modern alphabet gender movement strike us as a form of gnosis in which a wrong step excludes one from the gnostic elect? So-called conversion therapy is banned, as are attempts to dissuade children from 'transitioning'. It is forbidden to pray, counsel or protest within certain limits of abortion centres.[2] Professional sportsmen are excoriated for not wearing the 'Pride' badge or colours.

Furthermore, for two years, we have been brutalised and cowed by what Douglas Farrow calls 'hygienic gnosticism'.[3] The method to deal with COVID-19 was formulated by health bureaucrats as the only possible legitimate response to what was ultimately a prudential issue and enforced by the state,

---

1   Recent revelations that shoppers entering Kmart, Bunnings and The Good Guys unwittingly 'consent' to the use of facial recognition software are horrifying but on reflection not that surprising exemplifications of this phenomenon: Jarni Blakkarly, 'Kmart, Bunnings and The Good Guys using facial recognition technology in stores,' last updated 12 July 2022 at https://www.choice.com.au. Another example is the Victorian Government giving employers the ability to view their employees COVID-19 vaccination status: Flat White, 'RIP medical privacy,' 7 July 2022 at https://spectator.com.au.

2   C.f. the legislation considered in *Clubb v Edwards* (2019) 267 CLR 171.

3   See his 'A New Catholicism: The Eugenic Healthy Tyranny as a Test of Fidelity, Part I', 6 July 2022, and "Test of Fidelity", 9 July 2022, available from his Substack webpage (https://douglasfarrow.substack.com/). He considers that the absolutizing tendencies of the state in the modern period are rooted in 'Luther's two kingdoms doctrine'.

big business and media. Those who came to different views were shunned, ostracized and pushed to the margins.[1] Even presenting *legal* arguments questioning the *legality* of public health orders (as opposed to their merits) were verboten, as occurred when Linked-In removed an article by a NSW solicitor questioning the constitutional validity of NSW's public health orders.[2] During the COVID-19 pandemic, The Royal Society in Britain sought legislation that would punish '"those who produced and disseminated false information" about vaccines', measured against the monopolised scientific consensus on vaccines. As Sumption pointed out, it would only be a particular state or quasi-state authority that could declare what vaccine information was valid and those who disagreed would be punished.[3] People are simply *not allowed* to think differently, let alone express those thoughts, from the prevailing gnoses.

THE RELATIONSHIP BETWEEN FREEDOM OF SPEECH AND FREEDOM OF RELIGION

What to do about it?

The thought is that we need to build a culture in which there are practices of civilised and convivial inquiry that fearlessly pursue and are open to truth (and beauty and goodness). For this enterprise to be successful, the culture needs to recog-

---

[1] Proponents of the COVID-policy response might argue that the very nature of the problem required the state intervention that we saw; the concern is, however, with the costs of that approach precisely insofar as it removed opportunities to exercise spiritual freedom (not least in the closure of churches, synagogues, mosques, etc.) and limited personal responsibility, in order to pursue a highly reductionist and gnostic policy.

[2] A precise citation cannot be given because the web link to the argument was removed.

[3] 'Foreword' to Francis Hoar, *In Protection of Freedom of Speech: A Legal Analysis* (2021), p. 2.

nise that such pursuit and openness is the most important of human pursuits and thereby foster it.[1]

In this context, the relationship between freedom of speech and freedom of religion bears examination. A feature of contemporary gnostic attempts to suppress communication is, it is submitted, modernity's paradoxical relationship with capital-T and lower-t 'truth'. Embedded within contemporary gnosis is the particular epistemology that cannot bear the uncertainty embedded in philosophical inquiry and excludes religious truth as merely subjective, while simultaneously claiming the ability to know all things. It thereby privileges what we can only know relatively. But this inverts the proper order. Capital-T truth is the preserve of revealed religion and refers to what has been revealed to us by God (included here are claims about faith and morals such as the meaning of human sexuality), which, along with necessary philosophical truths, is the only thing about which we can ultimately be certain, because God can neither 'deceive nor be deceived'.[2] Even then, the mystery of God and His dealings with us cannot be exhaustively contained in human language, which while containing the truth, itself points to the ever-greater, inexhaustible God.

1   C.f. Heydon, pp. 195-196 on civility and the International Theological Commission's document, 'Religious Freedom for the Good of All: Theological Approaches and Contemporary Challenges', 21 March 2019, e.g. secs 67-69, available from https://www.vatican.va.

2   First Vatican Council, *Dei Filius*, 24 April 1870, III available from https://www.vatican.va; St Thomas Aquinas, *Summa Theologiae*, I, 1, 5: 'In both these respects, [the sacred] science surpasses other speculative sciences; in point of greater certitude, because other sciences derive their certitude from the natural light of human reason, which can err; whereas this derives its certitude from the light of the divine knowledge, which cannot be misled' (translation by the Fathers of the English Dominican Province (Notre Dame, IN: Ave Maria Press, 1981)).

Apart from revealed capital-T Truth, there is a vast realm of various lower-t truths about which there can be only varying degrees of certitude. Sumption correctly notes the provisional nature of most claims of knowledge: 'All statements of fact or opinion are provisional. They reflect the current state of knowledge and experience. But knowledge and experience are not closed or immutable categories'.[1] What contemporary society appears to lack is precisely the recognition that computer models, scientific hypotheses, political, economic and medical theories and opinions can only ever provisionally declare the truth. For this reason, such theories are always liable to be overturned at the next paradigm shift, whether it concerns matters such as whether humanity is about to enter another ice age (as suggested in 1970s) or be doomed by 'climate emergency' (as we are apparently now facing). However, it is precisely these truth-claims that are treated as Gospel truth by contemporary gnosis, and which therefore admit of no exceptions.

The claim that most truth-claims are provisional is not to claim that the pursuit of them is not important or that we are condemned to immobility on policy issues because we are always in pursuit of truth. It is to claim that epistemic humility is necessary to guard against the inquiry becoming totalitarian gnosis. The provisional character of these truth claims and the totalising dangers of centralising under the state the ability to determine them requires a robust culture of freedom of expression in which truth claims are tested. Such a culture is necessary in order that 'open discussion' be permitted to allow the 'search for truth'.[2] Particularly important is to build a

1   Sumption, 'Foreword,' p. 2.
2   *Coleman v Power* (2004) 220 CLR 1 at [333] per Heydon J quoting the appellant's submission. Speaking generally, legal protections ought to be applied and interpreted liberally, whether as an express constitutional liberty, as in the case of the US Constitution or the Uni-

culture that limits the ability of the state, bureaucracies and so on to police speech and impose penalties for the expression of heterodox views in the vast realm of prudential matters. To give these bodies a monopoly on truth in these matters is to fall into the gnostic trap of arrogating epistemic control to those who simply cannot know the full truth and whose own interests are often at stake. As MacIntyre says, we 'must treat the agencies of the state with unremitting suspicion'.[1] He argues cogently that the contemporary state, as a principal actor in society with its own interests, 'is not and cannot be evaluatively neutral' as between competing conceptions of the good and, because it is not, 'cannot generally be trusted to promote any worthwhile set of values, including those of autonomy and liberty'. He goes

---

versal Declaration of Human Rights, or fundamental common law right, which can only be abrogated with clear and necessary intendment: c.f. Heydon, op. cit., 343. See also *Monicilovic v R* (2011) 245 CLR 1 at [444] per Heydon J. There may be reasonable exceptions: e.g. *Comcare v Banerji* (2019) 267 CLR 373, e.g. per Edelman at [164]: 'in Australia the boundaries of freedom of speech are generally the province of parliament; the judiciary can constrain the choices of a parliament only at the outer margins for reasons of systemic protection'. However, compare *Clubb v Edwards* (2019) 267 CLR 171, which upheld the validity of Victorian and Tasmanian legislation prohibiting 'location-protests'. The submission of LibertyWorks Inc is persuasive: 'The practical operation of the provision is significantly to impact anti-abortion protesters and it is calculated to have a chilling effect on political communication in relation to anti-abortion concerns. Harassment and intimidation may characterise some picketing. However, the instant case involves peaceful protesting. The apprehended consequence of distress and anxiety is one of the purposes of any protest, but especially of location-protests. The law has privileged the feelings or states of mind of those accessing abortion clinics over the feelings and states of mind of those peacefully picketing abortion clinics. If there is to be a privileging, the freedom to protest in public is constitutionally privileged,' at pp. 184-185.

1   MacIntyre, op. cit., p. 213.

on to state that whomever it is that should determine the outer limits of acceptable speech, 'it should not be the agencies of the state'.¹ Better, he argues, is to allow the practice of the pursuit of truth itself to exclude what is outrageous or unacceptable.²

The claim about the importance of pursuing truth is underscored by the importance of the proclamation of religious truth. In over-emphasising provisional truth-claims, contemporary society fails to recognise the importance of religious truth precisely to draw us out of the immanentist, gnostic trap in which we find ourselves.³ Most especially does a culture of freedom of speech need to be understood as intrinsically connected to freedom of religion. It is striking, if adventitious, that the First Amendment rights recognised in the US Constitution include *together* the free exercise of religion and speech.⁴ Freedom of speech, it is submitted, should principally be un-

---

1   Ibid., p. 214. He also argues that 'representatives of insurance companies or of bureaucratic managers of healthcare organizations', because they have unavoidable conflicts of interest, should be excluded from discussions regarding the goods of health: p. 215.

2   Ibid., p. 214ff.

3   C.f. Pope Benedict XVI, "The Listening Heart: Reflections on the Foundations of Law," 22 September 2011, available from https://www.vatican.va: 'In its self-proclaimed exclusivity, the positivist reason which recognizes nothing beyond mere functionality resembles a concrete bunker with no windows, in which we ourselves provide lighting and atmospheric conditions, being no longer willing to obtain either from God's wide world. And yet we cannot hide from ourselves the fact that even in this artificial world, we are still covertly drawing upon God's raw materials, which we refashion into our own products. The windows must be flung open again, we must see the wide world, the sky and the earth once more and learn to make proper use of all this.'

4   The historical reasons for them being put together were because they were rights that the Federal Congress could not burden: Akhil Reed Amar, *America's Constitution: A Biography* (New York: Random House, 2005), pp. 319-320.

derstood as an instrumental freedom. Its end is not to permit communication for the sake of it, but to enable individuals to pursue and discover truth in its manifold splendour and as found in the varying contexts of human life and inquiry.[1] It is not an end in itself but for something greater.

That 'something greater' is the proclamation of religious truth as at the summit of the hierarchy of truth. Because freedom of speech is ordered to the truth, and because genuine religion proposes fundamental truths, freedom of speech is, at its most important, necessarily ordered to the higher order free exercise of religion and for that reason should generally be afforded great breadth of operation.[2] St John Paul II argued that freedom of religion is in fact the most important of human freedoms because, as Pope Benedict XVI pointed out, the human person is a spiritual being, 'relational and open to the transcendent'.[3] All rights flow from the recognition that the human person's dignity derives from being open to God and therefore each other as *persons*. The Second Vatican Council taught that human beings have the duty and the right 'to seek truth in religious matters', which must be done in accordance with our rational and social natures, 'by free enquiry with the help of teaching or instruction, communication and dia-

---

1   Evidence that this is so is that society does not and cannot grant its members absolute freedom of communication in all matters and all forms. As John Finnis points out, not even JS Mill attempted to claim as much. Finnis also provides a number of examples where the law prohibits unfettered speech: 'Freedom of Speech,' in *Reason in Action* (Oxford: Oxford University Press, 2011), p. 299. See also *Coleman v Power* at [185] per Gummow and Hayne JJ.

2   We could also suggest that freedom of speech in fact depends on the free exercise of religion to thrive.

3   International Theological Commission, 'Religious Freedom for the Good of All,' secs 24-25.

logue'.[1] Implicitly, the 'freedom ... from coercion in religious matters' extends to protection of freedom of speech, especially insofar as it permits persons to pursue religious truth.[2] A healthy society gives genuine religion room in its worship, preaching and interventions in the public square to propose absolute truth claims (including with respect to issues such as marriage, sex, family, sexual identity and so on), both as essential to the nature of genuine religion and to allow seekers of truth the capacity to discover it. A deeply unhealthy society – one which does not accord with the nature of human persons and their end – will exclude such communication, *as well as* robust discussions about what are ultimately prudential judgments, because these are themselves ordered to the pursuit of truth and valuable precisely for that reason.

BUILDING A CULTURE OF TRUTH: LIBERTY OF THE SPIRIT IS THE KEY TO FREEDOM

For a culture of freedom of inquiry and expression ordered to the pursuit of truth – including, fundamentally, openness to religious truth as revealed by God – to flourish, religion itself needs to be recognised and fostered. Both Dawson and Voegelin identified the apparent paradox whereby the increase in technical control and ability leads to spiritual and civilizational death. For Dawson to say 'there is an intimate relation between [a culture's] religious faith and its social achievement' is to recognise the accuracy of Voegelin's comment that 'the life of the spirit is the source of order in man and society'.[3]

1 *Dignitatis Humanae*, 7 December 1965, sec. 3, from *Vatican Council II, Volume 1: The Conciliar and Post-Conciliar Documents*, new revised edition, ed. Austin Flannery (Northport, New York/Dublin: Costello Publishing Co/Dominican Publications, 1996).
2 C.f. Second Vatican Council, *Dignitatis Humanae*, sec. 4.
3 Dawson, *Religion and the Rise of Western Culture*, p. 14, Voegelin,

Especially is the life of the spirit endangered when 'human energies are thrown into the great enterprise of salvation through world-immanent action', because doing so distances the protagonists from the life of the spirit.[1] A reordering of the West away from precipitous decline requires, then, the elimination of gnosis and space for the human spirit to breathe and for religious freedom and freedom of speech, especially in matters of fundamental truth, to be practised robustly and virtuously.[2]

Furthermore, if Dawson and Voegelin were correct, then anterior to the question of what legal shape protection of freedom of speech and, even more importantly, of religion, should take, is the question of the spiritual health of society, which in turn depends upon the health of the Catholic religion historically at the centre of Western civilisation. A theological solution as embodied in particular institutions in the life of the Church, therefore, is at the heart of any genuine attempt to reach a practical solution to the threats posed to freedom of speech and religion. Members of the Church cannot practice the virtue of truth-seeking unless the theological culture that nourishes them – indirectly or directly – itself avoids the epistemological pitfalls that Voegelin identifies. If it is true that Gnosticism – intrinsic to which is the claim that the only acceptable form of knowledge is that which fits within the particular intellectual system – undergirds totalitarian impulses to inhibit religious practice and chill speech, theologians are obligated to propose different *theological* methods and starting points in response. These starting points must tear apart and overcome the temptation to limit human knowledge to

---

New Science of Politics, p. 131.
1   Voegelin, *New Science of Politics*, p. 131.
2   C.f. Benedict XVI, 'The Listening Heart'. By this, it is not meant that religious truth itself is the product of inquiry but that practices in the pursuit of truth fosters the ability to accept its revelation.

what can be known empirically and which excludes religious knowledge as knowledge.

It is no surprise that Voegelin cites Hans Urs von Balthasar and Henri de Lubac in his discussion of Gnosticism.[1] These, along with Ratzinger, are principal examples of theologians who detected the dangers of gnosis to the theological enterprise. Arrayed against them were the *Concilium* school of post-conciliar theology. In its method, the school incorporated Kantian, Hegelian and Marxist philosophies. It sought to 'baptise' the secular and utilise those philosophies to foster intra-mundane eschatological projects, precisely that immanentisaton of the eschaton of which Voegelin wrote and which all bear the characteristics of gnosis. Far more consistent with the nature of revelation, it is submitted, is an analogical metaphysics, Augustinian-Aegidian view of the supernatural and Chalcedonian Christology, which recognise the sheer, dazzling priority of Christ. Christ is the 'concrete' *analogia entis*, the Incarnate Truth pointing to the ever-greater God, who relativises all human thought patterns and gnoses.[2]

At the centre of cultural development is theology (or a-theology), as embodied in the life of the Church, cultural practices and traditions in which there can be open, charitable and at times robust discussion. MacIntyre famously concluded his seminal *After Virtue* by arguing that the West was awaiting

---

1   Voegelin, *Science, Politics and Gnosticism*, p. xxi.

2   See the author's doctoral thesis: *The Hope and History Debate in Fundamental Theology* (Doctor of Philosophy (School of Philosophy and Theology)), University of Notre Dame Australia, 2020. https://researchonline.nd.edu.au/theses/283, Aidan Nichols, *Christendom Awake: On Reenergizing the Church in Culture* (Grand Rapids, Michigan: William B Eerdmans Publishing Company, 1999), p. 24 quoting Hans Urs von Balthasar, *Explorations in Theology I: The Word Made Flesh* (San Francisco: Ignatius Press, 1989), p. 177.

INTRODUCTION

'another – doubtless very different – St Benedict'.¹ MacIntyre considered that virtue was developed within particular cultural practices and traditions, and typical pursuits of modernity – such as bureaucratic administration – intrinsically inhibit the development of virtue.² Particular religious, cultural and practical forms need therefore to be established in order that the virtues of honesty, truth-telling and the proclamation of the Gospel are to be developed and practised; in other words to enable the Burkean attitude, which is the motto of the Centre, to be exercised.

In this context, special tribute must be paid to the Most Reverend Julian Porteous, Archbishop of Hobart. One of the author's great personal graces of the COVID-19 period was the discovery of Notre Dame Priory, located here in Tasmania. Through the dark days of isolation and lockdown, where the civility and conviviality necessary for the mutual, communal pursuit of truth were sorely tested by the ever-present temptation to gnosis, the liturgy and preaching of the monks were beacons of light and proclamation of fearless, uncomfortable but nourishing truth for people around the world.³ Vital for the future of the Church and society is precisely for these institutions such as these to be given the liberty and space by Church and secular authorities to worship, preach and engage in apostolate. In one, they embody true freedom of religion and expression.

---

1   Alasdair MacIntyre, *After Virtue*, 3rd ed. (Notre Dame, Indiana: University of Notre Dame Press, 2007), p. 263.

2   Tracey Rowland, *Catholic Theology* (London/New York: Bloomsbury, 2017), pp. 182-183.

3   E.g., 'God is Not Mocked', 5 September 2021: https://www.notredamemonastery.org/from-the-cloister/2021/9/5/beware-a-homily, the author has been informed, that has had over 19,000 visits.

CONCLUSION: THE EXAMPLE OF KRISTIN LAVRANSDATTER

This paper began by describing a passage in Sigrid Undset's great trilogy *Kristin Lavransdatter*. What saved the child from physical death and the men from spiritual death was the fearless truth telling of the nun, who denounced pagan barbarism, in light of the Gospel *and* as backed up by her bravery. When we face our judgment, may we not be found guilty of failing to exercise our God-given ability and duty to pursue and communicate truth and of keeping silent when we ought to have spoken up, and for failing to act with integrity of thought, speech and action.

FREE SPEECH AS 'OUROBOROS': SELF-DEVOURING FREEDOMS
Kenneth Crowther

ABSTRACT

G.K Chesterton wrote in Orthodoxy that "the virtues are let loose… wander more wildly, and the virtues do more terrible damage." Freedom of speech suffers from a similar fate. In a 'post-Christian secular age' that has largely shrugged off the burdensome impositions of natural hierarchy and has dislocated and redefined the virtues, what are the implications for freedom of speech? Over recent decades, as an essentially negative liberty it has found itself in the privileged position of eroding positive liberties. Obsession with the right to freedom of speech under the mantle of an unbridled liberalism has resulted in an 'ouroboros of freedoms' – freedoms which devour themselves as the snake eats its own tail. Through lessons from depictions of Satan in Paradise Lost and The Divine Comedy, this paper will ask what supporting virtues are needed to reposition freedom of speech in its proper place, and whether this is even possible.

RECLAIMING FREEDOM

IN THE FIRST book of John Milton's epic poem *Paradise Lost* the reader is hurled headlong into the fiery lake of Hell to witness the awakening of Satan. Laying 'vanquished, rolling in the fiery gulf, confounded though immortal'[1], surrounded by the flames of Hell, 'yet from those flames no light, but rather darkness visible serv[ing] only to discover sights of woe'[2], Satan proclaims the first of what will become many rebellious orations, the likes of which have led countless critics over the centuries to take his side, viewing him as the hero of the grand epic. After landing on a dreary plain, forlorn, wild and desolate, Satan glories to have escaped the lake, and proclaims to his companion, Beelzebub, one of the most famous passages of the poem:

> *Farewell happy fields*
> *Where joy for ever dwells: Hail horrors, hail*
> *Infernal world, and thou profoundest Hell*
> *Receive thy new possessor: One who brings*
> *A mind not to be changed by place or time.*
> *The mind is its own place, and in itself*
> *Can make a Heaven of Hell, a Hell of Heaven.*
> *What matter where, if I be still the same,*
> *And what I should be, all but less then he*
> *Whom thunder hath made greater? Here at least*
> *We shall be free; the Almighty hath not built*
> *Here for his envy, will not drive us hence:*
> *Here we may reign secure, and in my choice*
> *To reign is worth ambition though in Hell:*
> *Better to reign in Hell, than serve in Heaven.*[3]

---

1   Milton, J. *Paradise Lost*, Book 1, Lines 52-53.
2   Ibid., Book 1, Lines 62-64.
3   Ibid., Book 1, Lines 249-263.

It is my belief that these are some of the most profound, illuminating, and dangerous words ever written. And while it may not at first be apparent, they are words that hold an interesting relevance for freedom of speech. What I intend to demonstrate is that freedom is a slippery term, not only due to the contrasting definitions of negative and positive liberty, but also through the recognition that a certain definition of freedom is, to put it bluntly, satanic, and therefore when campaigning for freedom and the modern idea of the right to freedom of speech, we are treading the boundary between Heaven and Hell, and that if tempted to cross this threshold, like Dante, we should 'abandon all hope, we who enter here.'[1]

Such a dramatic opening—to imply 'satanic' connections—may suggest this paper intends to position itself against freedom of speech. That is not the case. As will be made clear, freedom, and indeed freedom of speech, are good things. But these good things can be misunderstood and disconnected from the source from whence their goodness stems, twisting them from their intended form. As G.K. Chesterton once wrote comparing virtues and vices, 'the virtues are let loose ... [and] wander more wildly, and the virtues do more terrible damage ... [They] have been isolated from each other and are wandering alone.'[2] Likewise, when freedom of speech is isolated from those virtues that should naturally accompany it, it too has the tendency to wreak havoc.

Returning then to Satan, many critics, emerging perhaps unsurprisingly from the dynamism and radicalism that typified the Romantic movement, have identified Satan as the true hero of *Paradise Lost*. The famous words of William Blake

1   Paraphrased from Alighieri, D. *The Divine Comedy: Inferno*, Canto III, Line 9.

2   Chesterton, G.K. *Orthodoxy*, (Chicago: Moody Publishers, 2009), p.50.

are that 'the reason Milton wrote in fetters when he wrote of Angels & God, and at liberty when he wrote of Devils & Hell, is because he was a true Poet and of the Devil's party without knowing it.'[1] The Poet Laureate Robert Southey[2], placed advocates of this response in the ignominiously titled 'Satanic School', a school that it could be argued still exists to this day, exemplified perhaps by Saul Alinsky's *Rules for Radicals*, which includes an introductory acknowledgement to, as he put it, 'the very first radical: from all our legends, mythology, and history ... the first radical known to man who rebelled against the establishment and did it so effectively that he at least won his own kingdom—Lucifer.'[3]

What is it in the character of Satan that radical thinkers such as Blake[4] and Alinsky find so attractive? My suggestion is that it is exactly Satan's use of the word 'free'. As Alinsky says, Satan has indeed 'won his own kingdom', at least, according to *his* perspective in his opening address to Beelzebub in which he claims that it is 'better to reign in Hell than serve in Heaven'. 'Here at least we shall be free,' he says.

Free. In Hell. After saying 'farewell to happy fields where joy forever dwells' and recognising that his new life will contain only despair; here, at least, he shall be free. This perplexing approach to the concept of freedom illustrates the problematic scope for the word's definition. Freedom means a great many things and is defined variously by a great many people. Satan's

    1   Blake, W. *The Marriage of Heaven and Hell.*
    2   de Montluzin, E.L. 'Southey's 'Satanic School' Remarks: An Old Charge for a New Offender', *Keats-Shelley Journal.* (Vol:21/22, 1972/1973), pp.29-33.
    3   Alinsky, S. *Rules for Radicals*, (New York: Vintage Books, 1990).
    4   I do not here intend to suggest that Blake was a purely 'Satanic' thinker. He held to an unorthodox Christianity resulting in poems as diverse in their theology as *The Lamb* and *The Everlasting Gospel.*

ideal freedom is defined in one specific way: merely by a lack of overt service to God—regardless of the fact that God is a benevolent, all powerful and loving leader. To bend the knee at all is, in Satan's mind, the great tragedy, and thus Satan's 'unconquerable will'[1] is seen as a heroic triumph.

While Satan-as-hero has been a mainline critical response for over two centuries, C.S. Lewis combatted it in *A Preface to Paradise Lost*, in which he points out that Satan is never happy, always unfulfilled, always in despair, always in torment, a truth also articulated powerfully in Stanley Fish's *Surprised by Sin*. In short, to see Satan as a heroic overcomer is to look at him through rose-coloured glasses. Satan is a liar, and he lies to himself and to the reader. As Lewis points out, Milton 'did not foresee that his work would one day meet the disarming simplicity of critics who take for gospel things said by the father of falsehood in public speeches to his troops.'[2]

These are indeed lies, and Satan, in his better moments—if the prince of darkness can have better moments—knows them to be lies. His torment is complete because he has made a hell for himself, and therefore he is always 'in Hell'. He recognises this upon journeying to Earth and reflecting on the love of heaven. 'Be then his love accursed' he says to himself, 'since love or hate, / To me alike, it deals eternal woe'. But immediately upon saying this he realises it is not love that should be accursed, but himself, 'since against [God's] will [Satan] / Chose freely what [he] now so justly rues.' He is miserable and knows he cannot escape his infinite despair. In a moment of blinding clarity, which he soon chooses to forget, Satan says, 'Which way I fly is Hell; myself am Hell.'[3] Such a recognition

1 Milton, J. *Paradise Lost*, Book 1, Line 106.
2 Lewis, C.S. *A Preface to Paradise Lost*, (New York: Oxford University Press, 1961), p.100.
3 Op. cit. Book 4, Lines 69-75.

makes perfect sense considering his initial proclamation to have brought a mind with him not to be changed by place or time. His mind goes with him wherever he is, and he has an illogical faith in its capacity to 'make a Heaven of Hell and a Hell of Heaven'. Unfortunately for Satan, he has only understood half of the equation. He cannot make a Heaven of Hell. But he can certainly make a Hell of Heaven, because he himself is Hell.

This is the all-important background when we remember that Satan believed in his freedom—he believed he had achieved it. He had not been free in Heaven and he now believes he has 'escaped' the rule of God. But this freedom is a poor imitation of true freedom. It is, in fact, only another form of servitude. Rather than serving God, he is instead enslaved to himself—enslaved, paradoxically, precisely by his desire for freedom.

This paradox is illustrated in that other great epic about Heaven and Hell, Dante's *Divine Comedy*, which paints an altogether less romantic picture of Satan. Rather than dynamically and charismatically assembling the hordes of demons in the halls of Pandemonium, whipping them into a frenzy before setting off courageously into the unknown to corrupt God's newest creation, Dante's devil is hopelessly inert.

As the poet and his guide Virgil journey to the bottom of hell they find themselves trekking the frozen river Cocytus, a strong cold wind blowing towards them as they make their way to its source. The river opens out into a wide lake in the centre of which the giant form of Lucifer sits frozen up to his waist in the ice, ceaselessly beating his wings in his attempt to escape:

> *Underneath each [arm] came forth two mighty wings,*
> *Such as befitting were so great a bird;*
> *Sails of the sea I never saw so large.*

> *No feathers had they, but as of a bat*
> *Their fashion was; and he was waving them,*
> *So that three winds proceeded forth therefrom.*
> *Thereby Cocytus wholly was congealed.*
> *With six eyes did he weep, and down three chins*
> *Trickled the tear-drops and the bloody drivel.*[1]

Satan remains frozen in this lake in his punishment, doomed for all eternity, and his three faces constantly weep tears as he struggles in vain to break free of the ice by the power of his giant wings. But of course, it is exactly that which keeps him frozen. The beating of those wings forces gales of wind down onto the lake, freezing it solid, and keeping him forever a prisoner of unyielding ice. It is his desire for freedom that keeps him captive. He is literally enslaved by his obsession with freedom on his terms. And that is the crux of the issue—those three words: on his terms. While at first Milton's Satan appears vastly different and heroically superior to Dante's, they are ultimately the same. Enslaved by their obsession with freedom on their terms, neither of them is free, neither of them will ever be free; and it is precisely because they are so obsessed with freedom that they will never achieve it.

This image forms the background of the following discussion of freedom of speech, which will address three distinct points. First, the difference between positive and negative liberty is largely undiscussed these days, but it is vital to recognise some of the pitfalls of obsessing over freedoms and rights in general. Second, Libertarianism and Liberalism have become strange bedfellows for Conservatism over recent decades; strange, because their interests only occasionally overlap, and unconstrained liberalism is counter to Conservatism and

1   Alighieri, D. *The Divine Comedy: Inferno*, Canto 34, Lines 46-54.

is in fact self-destructive. An effective metaphor is the ancient symbol of an ouroboros: the snake eating its own tail. Liberalism suffers from this self-destruction as one freedom devours all others, and we are faced, in the end, with what James Kalb called 'the tyranny of liberalism.'[1] Finally, I will suggest a potential remedy found firstly in recognising the right place of freedom of speech in a hierarchy of goods, and secondly by surrounding it by and defining it through the virtues, those long neglected and much maligned pointers to true reality.

We venture now into the territory of positive and negative liberty, and turn to *The Stanford Encyclopedia of Philosophy* for definitions:

> *Negative liberty is the absence of obstacles, barriers or constraints. One has negative liberty to the extent that actions are available to one in this negative sense. Positive liberty is the possibility of acting—or the fact of acting—in such a way as to take control of one's life and realize one's fundamental purposes.*[2]

The article goes on to give the illustration of a person driving on the road, choosing freely at each intersection to turn first left and then right. There are no other cars on the road and these choices therefore are made without obstacle or impediment. This is an example of negative freedom, as nothing was in the driver's way. However, the situation is seen in a different light if it is revealed that the driver is speeding to the store to buy a packet of cigarettes, deeply addicted, and knowing that the tobacconist will close any minute. Rather than driving,

---

[1] Kalb, J. *The Tyranny of Liberalism*, (Wilmington: ISI Books, 2008).

[2] Carter, I. 'Positive and Negative Liberty', *Stanford Encyclopedia of Philosophy*.

he feels like he is being driven. This is the distinction between negative and positive freedom: negative, because it implies the absence of something, that is, the absence of obstacles; positive, because it requires the presence of something, that is self-mastery or self-determination.

In our earlier Luciferian examples, therefore, Satan is celebrating a negative liberty. He has escaped the bonds of servitude to God, or so he deceives himself into thinking. However, he has not discovered any form of positive liberty. He is instead driven internally further into himself, further into Hell and despair. Dante's depiction is even clearer. Satan's wings illustrate exactly the competition between these two forms of liberty. They beat to be free: a desire for negative freedom. Their beating keeps him enslaved: a lack of positive freedom.

Therefore, by pursuing only negative freedom, one ends up caught between these two competing forms of freedom, resulting in a stagnant, despairing, stasis. It is my contention that until these distinctions are accounted for, our society too will be stuck between these conceptions of liberty. In fact, it is exactly where we find ourselves today. Never arriving at any kind of true freedom, rather, suffering like Satan, our desire to be free enslaves us. As the ouroboros devours its own tail, our freedoms consume themselves.

And there is a good reason for this. It is because certain conceptions of freedom are impossible. If we, like Satan, are sloppy with our terms, there simply is no such thing as pure, complete, unimpeded freedom. For in what way can a human possibly, ever, be entirely free? We are born into a world of limitations, for to be human is to be limited.[1] Even within the domain of

---

[1] This is precisely what advocates of the transhumanist movement rebel against, our natural limitations. A transhumanist of the 20th Century, a man who renamed himself FM2030, famously said, 'If it is natural to die then the hell with nature. Why submit to its tyranny? We

Christian theology, in which concepts of freedom such as the freedom found in Christ are commonplace, negative freedom, that is, to be completely unimpeded by any obstruction or limitation, is impossible. We are created beings and as such are subject to our creator, living within the limitations natural to our createdness. As Romans 9:20-21 states, 'But who are you, O man, to answer back to God? Will what is moulded say to its moulder, "Why have you made me like this?" Has the potter no right over the clay?' For while Jesus promises freedom, it is caught up in that beautiful mystery, the wisdom of God that is folly to the world, the seeming contradiction that to gain our lives we must lose them. To become our true selves, we must stop seeking ourselves, and to be truly free we must become bond slaves of Christ.

If it is freedom that we yearn for most—if we place it upmost in our hierarchy of goods—we will always be caught between these two conceptions of freedom, beating our wings in the ice. And thus, there are undoubtedly problems lurking within the concept of freedom of speech. On the one hand, it is a valuable and necessary condition of the harmonious life of the *polis*. On the other, it was, at least in part, exercising this freedom that transformed Lucifer to Satan.

It would be taking an overly simplistic view to refuse to recognise some of the inherent contradictions that lie at the heart of this topic. For example, one can reflect on statements by Campbell Newman[1] who stood for the senate under the Liberal Democrats in the lead-up to the 2022 election. Their website contains their 'Freedom Manifesto', which includes the need

---

must rise above nature. We must refuse to die.' C.S Lewis' *The Abolition of Man* and *That Hideous Strength* both speak powerfully to the dangers of the desire to escape all limitations.

1   Newman was interviewed by Jonathan Cole on the podcast *The Political Animals*, 10 April 2022.

for a free speech constitutional amendment. This is what it says:

> *Free speech is too important to be left to the whim of politicians. The Liberal Democrats would campaign to add the following to the Australian Constitution: Parliament shall make no law respecting an establishment of religion, or prohibiting the free exercise thereof; or abridging the freedom of speech, or of the press; or the right of the people peaceably to assemble, and to petition the Government for a redress of grievances.*[1]

As good as this may sound, it must also be pointed out that Newman's liberalism is nothing if not consistent. When he was questioned about his liberal credentials, which were perhaps rightly to be doubted considering his crackdown on motorcycle gangs when he was premier of Queensland, he responded by pointing out that his liberalism is particularly evident in social issues. He responded by saying, 'My attitude is that I don't want people to tell me how to live my life, that's why I backed gay marriage when I was the leader of the opposition in the LNP. That's why I've backed voluntary assisted dying … I don't know why people feel they have the right to tell other people how to live their lives.' Of course, he did later in the interview follow this up with the fact that he supports 'a Judeo-Christian bedrock of our government, our law, our business culture', but did not define what that really meant.

What we see here is the unfortunately common result of liberalism. Freedom is simply not specific enough—I would argue, not *good* enough—to be one's main cause. This is because inevitably and unescapably, soon enough one freedom will be forced up against another in a winner-takes-all fight to the death. At the end of such a competition, one of the two

[1] https://www.ldp.org.au/freedom.

competing freedoms will be destroyed.

This is a point that campaigners for new freedoms repeatedly reject during their campaigns. For example, it was consistently denied throughout the same-sex marriage debate that this new freedom extended to same-sex attracted people would have any impact upon religious people. In a 2015 article in *The Australian*, then Australian Human Rights Commissioner Tim Wilson wrote:

> *In advancing equality before the law, religious freedom must also be preserved. Doing so will ensure any reform does not become a Trojan horse for legally enforced anti-religious secularism. Some people wrongly argue that religious freedom ends at the temple door. It doesn't, in the same way sexual orientation doesn't end at the bedroom door.*
>
> *But a necessary precondition for your rights being respected is that you must respect the rights of others. If religious Australians want the law to preserve religious marriage and be free to act consistent with their conscience, then they can't concurrently deny same-sex couples a civil marriage.*[1]

These are interesting statements to reflect upon five years after the legalising of same-sex marriage. Wilson's belief that it would be possible to create a law in which 'neither side [gets] everything they want... because accommodating competing human rights isn't a zero-sum game'[2] has proven to be false. His suggestion that 'same-sex couples would be able to marry and others would be free to define marriage according to their faith or conscience without fear of legal retribution'[3] is being

---

1   Wilson, T. 'Same-sex marriage: a law that protects the rights of all parties', *Australian Human Rights Commission*, 8 August 2015.
2   Ibid.
3   Ibid.

proven false time and time again, such as the nine months of legal action taken against Archbishop Porteous and the 'Don't Mess with Marriage' booklet in 2016. Accommodating competing human rights, it would seem, is in fact a zero-sum game. When freedoms compete, someone always wins. So now that Newman believes so intently in freedom of religion and freedom of speech, I wonder if he recognises that his vote in favour of same sex marriage contributed to the erosion of those very freedoms for which he now fights? It seems very difficult to have it both ways.

These examples highlight the complicated reality of freedom of speech. In fact, in our contemporary post-modern world, freedom of speech becomes even more difficult to pin down because speech itself has lost its meaning. Not only are we dealing with a desire for freedom which is almost, if not entirely, impossible, but it is combined with the philosophy of metaphysical nominalism[1], a philosophy that has completely eroded the meaning of words and speech itself.

For what can freedom of speech possibly mean in a world where speech is meaningless and words can change definitions on a whim? This is entirely what we have seen upon reflection of the last few decades. Once a sworn enemy of conservatives, Germaine Greer now may find herself branded a 'Trans-Exclusionary Radical Feminist' or 'TERF' and may be surprised to find herself in the trenches fighting alongside conservatives in a rejection of new forms of radical gender-theory. For the current class of ruling elite, freedom of speech no longer has anything to do with speech. Due to the redefining power of nominalism, freedom of speech has transformed into freedom of will. Our modern world believes that our words have the

1 For more about the impacts of nominalism, see Crowther, K. 'Whose Culture, Which Liberal Arts?' in Daintree, D. (ed) *Passing on the Faith* (2022).

power to shape and change reality. We have bought the satanic lie that 'the mind is its own place'.

This is how and why liberalism has become a tyranny. As James Kalb writes:

> *To say there is a tyranny of liberalism is to say that a particular way of understanding political, social, and moral life, one that treats freedom, equality, and satisfaction of preferences as final standards, has become overwhelmingly dominant ... Liberal assumptions and ideas cause social authorities to lose touch with human reality, to supplant and suppress informal and traditional institutions such as the family, and eventually to overreach and become tyrannical, self-contradictory, and self-destructive.*[1]

This is the ouroboros. It is self-destructive because the obsession with any form of freedom, when disconnected from reality, will become naturally competitive. And freedom of speech will always result in questioning 'whose freedom?'. Take the May 2022 expulsion of Bernie Finn from the Liberal party—a more fitting example of the ouroboros perhaps cannot be found, than a liberal party expelling someone for exercising their liberty.

Despite all this negativity, there is an inherent goodness that undergirds the concept of freedom of speech. To discover it, an attempt could be made to place freedom within Thomas Aquinas' hierarchy of the goods, as detailed in his *Summa Theologiae*. Goodness, he writes, 'is predicated chiefly of the virtuous; then of the pleasant; and lastly of the useful.'[2] These have become known as his three types of good. Where, then, should we place freedom? Perhaps it encompasses all three, in

1 Op. cit. p.1.
2 Aquinas, T. *Summa Theologiae*, First Part, Question 5, Article 6.

that freedom is useful for achieving pleasure and virtue, and it is pleasurable to exercise and to live within freedom. But if we were to grant this, we must also grant that it is not negative freedom that is required for the fulfilment of virtue. All the cardinal virtues (fortitude, justice, temperance and prudence) can occur in the absence of negative freedom—that is, they can occur when obstacles to our free action are present. In fact, one may argue that negative freedom creates an even greater opportunity for virtue, such as an in an individual who finds themselves wrongly imprisoned and thus has an increased potential to display fortitude or charity. Positive freedom, on the other hand, *is* required. We must have received that gift of self-mastery; we must not be beholden to any animal urge or instinct that drives us uncontrollably forward. Therefore, for freedom to be accurately located within the scope of goods, it is not negative freedom, but positive freedom, that is required.

What has taken place, or at least, what well-meaning liberal-minded conservatives can be at risk of, is misplacing freedom, and instead of seeing it as a necessary condition for virtue, rather, seeing it as virtue itself. It is possible to inadvertently call a good thing the best thing, to mistake the means for the end, and thus to run the risk of seeing liberty—and even more problematically negative liberty—as a virtue, as a good in and of itself. And a result of this is the diminishing of the necessary conditions for human flourishing. We have not—it is important to note, lost the necessary conditions for virtue, for they can never be lost, but we are seeing freedom-obsession erode our capacity for those other goods of usefulness and pleasure.

It is quite possible that some of those individuals that pursued freedom of speech over the last few decades have been those that paved the way for the gradual erasure of other freedoms. Writing in 2017, John Anderson noted that 'sadly, the slavish pursuit of equality produces only slaves to equality, and slaves are no longer free; such is the paradox of good intention uninformed by history.'[1] Because the satanic ideal of freedom is an impossible lie, it will always lead to further lies. As James Kalb says:

> *The incremental style of liberalism obscures the radicalism of what it eventually demands and enables it always to present itself as moderate. What is called progress—in effect, movement to the left—is thought normal in present-day society, so to stand in its way, let alone to try to reverse accepted changes, is thought radical and divisive. We have come to accept that what was inconceivable last week is mainstream today and altogether basic tomorrow.*[2]

To return to our illustration of Satan, this self-contradictory and self-devouring nature of the pursuit of freedom is discussed in Lewis' *Preface to Paradise Lost*. The similarities are clear:

> *He wants hierarchy and does not want hierarchy. Throughout the poem he is engaged in sawing off the branch he is sitting on, not only in the quasi-political sense ... but in a deeper sense still, since a creature revolting against a creator is revolting against the source of his own powers—including even his power to revolt.*[3]

What, then, maybe be a solution to this complex problem? There is at least one, but like all solutions, it can be neither easy, nor quick. To return to Chesterton's observation: 'the virtues [are] let loose... [and] wander more wildly, and the

1   Anderson, J. 'Same-sex marriage survey sees freedom for all lost in the post', *The Australian*, 10 November 2017.
2   Op. cit. p.6.
3   Op. cit. p.96.

virtues do more terrible damage … [They] have been isolated from each other and are wandering alone.' As has been demonstrated, freedom of speech has suffered from a similar fate. In a 'post-Christian secular age' that has largely shrugged off the burdensome impositions of natural hierarchy and has dislocated and redefined the virtues, we must identify what freedom truly is, where it sits in the natural hierarchy, and what is needed to surround it for it to find its right place.

In Saint Augustine's *Confessions*, he speaks of virtue as *ordo amoris* or 'ordered affection'. Sin is disordered affection, loving things in the wrong way, the wrong degree, or at the wrong times. Freedom is a good thing, but if it is loved and pursed in a disorderly manner it will like all good things become corrupted, and then take on the characteristics of a vice. Freedom is not a virtue. Rather it is a state of being that will only manifest through the virtues. Therefore, the vital first principle of liberty is positive liberty. Yes, we need negative liberties. But without positive liberty, negative liberty will always enslave us. Positive liberty is that which breaks the loop of the ouroboros and sets us truly free.

The images of Satan in the ice or the driver yearning for his tobacco illustrate that positive liberty comes from an internal freedom. It is not about rejecting limitations, but, counterintuitively, embracing them. That is the difference between Satan and the Angels, they embrace the limitations of servitude to God and are blessed with joy as they fulfil their *telos*. For this is exactly what the virtues are—limitations which are good for us, limitations that set us free. And so, in a world which has rejected limitations we should not be surprised that the virtues have become dislocated and despised, and therefore to see freedom of speech wandering wildly and doing damage. The reckless rejection of virtue coupled with an obsession with freedom is essentially anti-hierarchical. But breaking all hierarchy ultimately means the erosion of all distinctions, all differences, and then the erosion of all value, which in turn creates a terrible meaningless flatland.

Where does this leave us? We are right to fight for freedom of speech. But we must also accept that in a world that has rejected virtue, what it looks like and how it should, and will, be used, is a contested, complex, and often contradictory space. The solution is to recognise that freedom of speech is a good thing. But it is not the best thing. And unless it finds its place in the hierarchy of reality; unless it is surrounded by fortitude, justice, temperance and prudence; unless it is used in the pursuit of truth, beauty and goodness; unless we endeavour not only to speak the truth, but to speak the truth in love, it will result, in the end, doing nothing more than keeping us enslaved, bringing Hell with us wherever we go.

REPRESSIVE TOLERANCE: ENFORCING MIND CONTROL AND GROUP THINK
Kevin Donnelly

ABSTRACT

As a result of Herbert Marcuse's concept of repressive tolerance we live in a time when freedom of speech and religion are regularly vilified and attacked. Marcuse argues, such is the oppressive and exploitive nature of Western societies like Australia, that those intent on radically overthrowing the status quo are free to use whatever means necessary to effect change. Freedom of speech and religion are not inherently worthwhile or valuable as they are key elements in what Althusser describes as the ideological state apparatus employed to reinforce the power of the ruling elites and dominate those less privileged.

'But if thought corrupts language, language can also corrupt thought' (George Orwell).

RECLAIMING FREEDOM

THE TITLE OF this presentation draws on an essay written by the Marxist academic Herbert Marcuse in which he argues such is the oppressive and exploitive nature of Western, capitalist societies cultural-left activists have the right to employ any and all means, no matter how unacceptable, to overthrow the status quo and radically change society. Tolerance is re-defined as intolerance with Marcuse arguing 'The conclusion reached is that the realisation of the objective of tolerance would call for intolerance toward prevailing policies, attitudes and opinions and the extension of tolerance towards policies, attitudes and opinions which are outlawed of suppressed'.[1] While Marcuse's essay was published in 1965, the underlying rationale and philosophy can be traced to the *Manifesto of the Communist Party*[2] published in 1848 and written by Karl Marx and Frederick Engels.

The *Manifesto* provides a revolutionary critique of advanced, industrial Western societies and what Marx and Engels describe as 'modern bourgeois society'.[3] The fathers of communism write 'The history of all hitherto existing society is the history of class struggles'[4] and 'modern bourgeois society has not done away with class antagonisms. It has but established new classes, new conditions of oppression, new forms of struggle in place of the old ones'.[5]

Since the time the *Manifesto* was published it is important to note the left's attack on Western societies has become more

---

1 Herbert Marcuse. 'Repressive Tolerance'. https://www.marcuse.org/herbert/publications/1960s/1965-repressive-tolerance-full-text.html Accessed 21 July 2022.
2 The Communist Manifesto. Published in China Mieville's *A Spectre Haunting Europe*. London. Head Zeus. 2022. P 190.
3 Ibid. P 190.
4 Ibid. P 189.
5 Ibid. P190.

strident and all encompassing. Whereas classical Marxism focuses on analysing the modes and means of production what has become known as cultural Marxism centres on a far wider analysis of society's social, political and cultural institutions and way of life. Michael Gove argues Marxism was reconceptualised as "primarily a cultural rather than an economic movement".[1] Gove writes "In place of anger at traditional capitalism, scorn was directed at the reigning values of the West".[2] The Marxist academic Louis Althusser's concept of the ideological state apparatus illustrates one of the defining features of cultural Marxism. Althusser argues capitalist society maintains dominance by ensuring institutions including schools, universities, the church, family and political, legal and cultural systems enforce the ruling ideology by conditioning citizens to accept as beneficial what is exploitive. As such, if the revolution is to be successful, activists have to infiltrate and take the long march through the institutions.[3]

The critique developed by Marx and Engels still dominates much of the cultural-left's analysis of Western, capitalist societies like Australia. Critics champion revolutionary change on the basis society is riven with inequality and oppression where the wealthy and privileged dominate and exploit the less advantaged and the dispossessed. Recent campaigns by LGBTIQ+ activists to re-define marriage and sexuality and the Black Lives Matter's argument society is awash with structural

1   Michael Gove. *Celsius 7/7*. London. Weidenfield & Nicolson. 2006. P 64.

2   Ibid. P 64.

3   Roger Kimball notes while the phrase 'the long march' is often attributed to Antonio Gramsci the expression was popularised by the German radical Rudi Dutschke during the rise of the New Left and the student riots of the late 60s and early 70s. See Roger Kimball. *The Long March*. San Francisco. Encounter Books. 2000.P 15.

racism and white supremacism can be traced to the *Manifesto*. The way what Sydney's Archbishop Fisher describes as 'absolutist secularism'[1] strives to banish Christianity from the public square and deny religious freedom of conscience and freedom of speech is also motivated by Marxism. The Italian Marxist Antonio Gramsci describes 'socialism as the religion destined to kill Christianity'.[2]

As a result, in addition to Western societies being condemned for being classist, society is attacked for being sexist, racist, heteronormative, homophobic and guilty of white supremacism and Eurocentrism. At the same time as condemning Western societies like Australia, the cultural-left portrays itself as a beacon of equality, freedom and liberty. Only the left is committed to ending intolerance and discrimination and able to build a worldly utopia where all are guaranteed freedom.

History proves otherwise. Since Russia's communist revolution in 1917 Marxism under its various guises has led to oppression, violence and the starvation, torture and death of countless millions. Best illustrated by Big Brother and The Party in George Orwell's dystopian novel *1984*, Marxism also stifles freedom of conscience and freedom of speech by enforcing mind control and group think. Whether rewriting history, controlling language, enforcing what Orwell describes as doublethink or denying and punishing disagreement and debate,

---

1 Archbishop Anthony Fisher OP. 'Archbishop Fisher on Secularism and Religion Today.' Published in *The Catholic Weekly* 22 August 2018. https://www.catholicweekly.com.au/archbishop-fisher-on-secularism-and-religion-today/ Accessed 21 July 2022.

2 Antonio Gramsci. 'Audacia e fede' in *Avanti*, 22 May 1916 quoted by Augusto Del Noce 'Notes of Secularization and Religious Thought' in *'The Crisis in Modernity'*. Canada. McGill-Queen's University Press. 2014. P 273.

the cultural-left is unforgiving and doctrinaire.

Such is the potency and prevalence of cultural Marxism, and its most recent iterations political correctness and cancel culture, barely a week goes by without yet another example of an idea, a book, a television show, a movie or an organisation or person being cancelled. Australian examples include the cartoonist Bill Leak for daring to reveal the dysfunctional nature of many Indigenous remote communities and Archbishop Porteous, Israel Folau and Margaret Court for espousing a Christian view of marriage and sexuality. Australia's Barry Humphries has also suffered as a result of arguing against transgenderism based on the belief sexuality is biologically determined.

Significant, such is the pervasive and doctrinaire nature of political correctness and cancel culture even those characterised as left-of-centre are under attack. The American non-gendered, radical feminist Camille Paglia writes 'We are now plunged once again into an ethical chaos where intolerance masquerades as tolerance and where individual liberty is crushed by the tyranny of the group'.[1] A second example involves Bari Weiss, a journalist considered progressive and working at the New York Times, who felt pressured to resign because of the accusation she was guilty of 'Wrongthink'.[2]

Additional evidence of the reaction against the inflexible nature of cultural-left censorship is the open letter signed by 150 authors, writers and public figures published in Harper's Magazine.[3] After warning of the dangers of right-wing ideo-

---

1 Camille Paglia. *Free Woman Free Men Sex Gender Feminism*. New York. Pantheon Books. 2017. P X

2 Barie Weiss' resignation letter can be found at https://www.bariweiss.com/resignation-letter Accessed 26 July 2022.

3 Harper's Magazine. 'A Letter on Justice and Open Debate'. July 7 2020. https://harpers.org/a-letter-on-justice-and-open-debate/

logical conformity illustrated by Donald Trump's election as President, the letter states 'But resistance must not be allowed to harden into its own brand of dogma or coercion—which right-wing demagogues are already exploiting. The democratic inclusion we want can be achieved only if we speak out against the intolerant climate that has set in on all sides'.

While cancel culture is relatively recent the origins of the left's intolerance, especially targeting Christianity, can be traced to Lenin's argument any action, no matter how reprehensible, is justified if it furthers the revolutionary cause. When warning about the dangerous and destructive nature of Marxism the Italian philosopher and cultural critic, Augusto Del Noce, refers to Lenin's statement 'Morality is whatever brings about the success of the proletarian revolution'.[1] Such is the unethical and amoral nature of Marxism Del Noce concludes 'every kind of violence, every ruse, every illegal action, every dissimulation, and every deception is licit if they are deemed to be necessary to reach the goal'.[2]

History proves how evil and destructive Marxism has been since the time of the Russian revolution. Untold millions were imprisoned, tortured, starved and killed by Stalin, Mao and as a result of Pol Pot's return to Year Zero. Such extreme examples are in addition to Marxist inspired strategies like re-writing history, censoring debate, denying freedom of expression and enforcing language control and group think.

The tile of this Colloquium is 'Freedom of Speech and Religion – The Essence of Western Civilisation' and an essay titled 'Repressive Tolerance' by Herbert Marcuse provides the most explicit account of why Marxism and its recent offshoot cancel culture represent an existential threat to freedom of conscience

---

Accessed 26 July 2022.
1   Augusto Del Noce. 'Op Cit. P 79.
2   Ditto. P 171.

and freedom of expression. During the 1920s a number of Marxist academics established the Frankfurt School in Germany dedicated to championing cultural-Marxism as a way to infiltrate and take control of the West's cultural and social institutions. Along with many other academics involved, including Theodore Adorno and Wilhelm Reich, Marcuse argues Western, capitalist societies are corrupt and guilty of oppressing the marginalised and disadvantaged.

In particular, Marcuse argues the existence of tolerance in Western societies 'strengthens the tyranny of the majority'.[1] As a result, Marcuse argues 'what is proclaimed and practiced as tolerance today, is in many of its most effective manifestations serving the cause of oppression'. As noted by Jennifer Oriel in her chapter in *Cancel Culture and the Left's Long March*:

> Marcuse argued for a new form of inequality won by censoring dissent. He wrote a "subversive majority" could be established by "undemocratic means" including "the withdrawal of toleration of speech and assembly" from groups that dissented from left-wing politics. He proposed "rigid restrictions on ... educational institutions" and "intolerance toward scientific research" that did not support his proposed revolutionary aims.[2]

During the late 1960s and early 1970s Western nations experienced a cultural revolution exemplified by the rise of the youth counter-culture movement, Vietnam moratoriums, the birth control pill, sexual liberation and the emergence of

1   Marcuse. Op Cit. https://www.marcuse.org/herbert/publications/1960s/1965-repressive-tolerance-fulltext.html Accessed 21 July 2022.

2   Jennifer Oriel. 'Universities' in Kevin Donnelly (editor) *Cancel Culture and the Left's Long March*. Melbourne. Wilkinson Publishing. 2021. P 58.

a rainbow alliance of radical philosophies and theories. Such theories, including postmodernism, deconstructionism and post-colonial, gender and sexuality theories, represent a strident and pervasive attack on Western civilisation and societies like Australia. While often in disagreement, what all hold in common is the belief rationality and reason no longer apply as such concepts are Eurocentric, binary and instrumental in oppressing the 'other'. In the same way tolerance is condemned as part of the state's ideological apparatus employed to reinforce power and privilege; civility and objectivity are also criticised as reinforcing inequality and injustice.

As a result, free and open discussion and debate are replaced by language control and group think. Much like Orwell's dystopian novel *1984*, where Big Brother and the Party rule, any who question or challenge the prevailing orthodoxy are silenced. Critical reasoning, once taught in schools as clear thinking, is replaced by emotion, hyperbole and ad hominem attacks and freedom of conscience and freedom of expression cancelled. As argued Christopher Lasch:

> *Once knowledge is equated with ideology, it is no longer necessary to argue with opponents on intellectual grounds or to enter into their point of view. It is enough to dismiss them as Eurocentric, racist, sexist, homophobic – in other words, as politically suspect.*[1]

As damaging is the reality, once rationality and reason no longer apply and freedom of expression denied, the only alternatives are epistemological suicide or violence. Evidence such is the case includes the increasing prevalence of what Orwell

---

1   Christopher Lasch. *Revolt of the Elites and the Betrayal of Democracy*. New York. Norton & Company. 1996. P 12.

calls 'Doublethink' – described as accepting two ideas at once without realising they are contradictory. Such is the power of indoctrination and mind control in the world of *1984* citizens accept without question 'war is peace, freedom is slavery and ignorance is strength'. Marcuse's argument equating tolerance with intolerance is yet another example of doublethink as is the argument the best way to promote liberty and freedom is to cancel any who think differently and who fail to conform. If it's impossible to settle arguments and disagreements rationally and by being objective and impartial it's also true violence is often the alternative. As argued by Mao 'political power grows out of the barrel of a gun'.

There's no doubt cancel culture is increasingly prevalent but, at the same time, there is evidence more and more people and various organisations are reasserting the primacy of rational argument and debate based on reason, logic and civility. In Australia, the Sydney based Campion College and the Ramsay Centre for Western Civilisation are committed to education being impartial and objective and teaching students the value of critical thinking and reasoned dialogue and debate. In America there are numerous liberal/arts colleges dedicated to the same objective and bodies like the Heterodox Academy and the National Association of Scholars are also beacons of common sense. In England, academics including Frank Furedi, Douglas Murray and the late Roger Scruton have entered the public square in their campaign to warn about the dangers of doctrinaire group think and the failure to tolerate dissenting opinions.

Given the often extreme and unforgiving nature of cancel culture it is also true more and more citizens are becoming aware of the dangers of woke ideology. A 2019 national survey organised by the ABC found 68% of those who responded felt political correctness had gone too far.[1] Such is the influence of cancel culture a third survey titled 'Measuring Social Inclusion' found 3 in 5 respondents believe 'white Australians' are victims of discrimination to some extent.[2] In 2022 a survey managed by Mark McCrindle found one-in-four Australians are afraid to freely express themselves in relation to controversial issues including abortion, religion and the environment.[3]

1 See https://www.abc.net.au/news/2019-11-28/australia-talks-annabel-crabb-political-correctness-analysis/11742380
2 Monash University & Behaviour Works Australia. 2020. 'Measuring Social Inclusion: The Inclusive Australia Social Inclusion Index'. https://inclusive-australia.s3.amazonaws.com/files/IA0013_Inclusive-Australia_Index2020_v6_single-pg-1.pdf
3 Mark McCrindle. 'The Cancel Culture and Acceptance in Australia – Exploring Australians' Acceptance of Others and their Worldview'. Reported by The Australian https://www.theaustralian.com.au/commentary/very-worrying-young-australians-fear-expressing-true-views-amid-cancel-culture/video/ab1211f56d3e2ab76154eedba6bdc498

HOW SAFE ARE RELIGIOUS EXEMPTIONS IN ANTI-DISCRIMINATION LAW?

Monica Doumit

ABSTRACT

Prior to the federal election, the then-Labor opposition laid out its plans for anti-discrimination law. If these pre-election undertakings are maintained, we can expect the newly-elected Labor Government to attempt to combine all federal anti-discrimination laws into a single piece of legislation, to refer the matter of religious exemptions in anti-discrimination law to the Australian Law Reform Commission, and to seek to protect LGBT students and teachers from discrimination while simultaneously maintaining the right of faith-based schools to teach religious doctrine and preference staff of the same faith. Given Labor will need to rely on the Greens in the Senate to pursue its legislative agenda, how realistic are any protections for religious individuals and institutions? What should we be doing now to prepare for all religious exemptions to anti-discrimination law being removed?

BEFORE I BEGIN on how safe or otherwise the religious exemptions are, I want to begin by briefly reminding us all of why they are so important.

In particular, I want to speak about the centrality of religious exemptions to the exercise of religious freedom.

When we talk about religious freedom, we are simultaneously speaking about two different ideas and two different legal realities.

There is the protection against discrimination on the basis of religious belief and activity, which is what is covered by most state and territory anti-discrimination legislation and what was sought to be protected by the failed *Religious Discrimination Bill 2022* (Cth). While not wanting to understate its importance, this isn't the most pressing issue of concern today and I don't presume do spend any time with it in the main body of this paper. We can return to it in the discussion if you like.

Instead, what I would like to speak about is what is referred to as *positive* religious freedom, that is, the freedom to engage in religious beliefs and practices. The United Nations Human Rights Committee lists some of these, saying religious freedom includes liturgies, the observance of dietary regulations, wearing of distinctive clothing, and the freedom to choose religious leaders and teachers, establish seminaries or religious schools, and prepare and distribute religious publications and texts[1].

In other words, religious freedom is not only personal and private, but it is supposed to be exercised communally, institutionally. Australian law does very little to recognise or protect this type of religious freedom. When it does so, it is generally by way of exemptions to existing anti-discrimination laws.

For example, the federal *Sex Discrimination Act 1984* prohibits discrimination on the basis of sex, sexual orientation, gender identity, marital status, pregnancy and more, but contains a broad based exemption for religious organisations that allows, for example, the Catholic Church to insist on a celibate, male priesthood. It also allows us to ensure that staff in Christian schools do not enter into same-sex marriages or decide to transition their gender and maintain their existing position,

---

1   UN Human Rights Committee (HRC), CCPR General Comment No. 22: Article 18 (Freedom of Thought, Conscience or Religion), 30 July 1993, CCPR/C/21/Rev.1/Add.4, available at: https://www.refworld.org/docid/453883fb22.html

particularly if it is a leadership position.

Similar exemptions exist in state-based anti-discrimination laws, with the key effect being that allowing religious institutions to choose their staff, ensuring that they not only claim a religious belief but – through their actions and lifestyle – live as if they believe it to be true.

The importance of these exemptions to the exercise of religious freedom cannot be understated, particularly when it comes to maintaining the communal and institutional aspect of religious freedom.

As the saying goes, personnel is policy. Without faithful personnel, and without the legal exemptions allowing us to employ them, we cannot maintain the faith-based nature of our institutions. We become what Pope Francis calls compassionate NGOs[1].

These exemptions have been in place largely since these anti-discrimination laws commenced, but it is only recently that we have seen them being challenged. 10 years ago, we saw the beginnings of a Royal Commission into Institutional Responses to Child Sexual Abuse. That lasted for five years and in the five years since that time – when the voice of Churches and religious institutions has been publicly weakened – we have seen a wave of social legislation that has encroached upon previously uncontroversial freedoms.

Same-sex marriage. Abortion until birth and associated buffer zones. Euthanasia. Laws prohibiting so-called conversion therapy and abolishing protections for the confessional seal. Each of these laws trespass on previously uncontroversial and largely uncontested exemptions for religious institutions

---

1   Pope Francis, Homily, "*Missa Pro Ecclesia*" with the Cardinal electors, 14 March 2013, available at: https://www.vatican.va/content/francesco/en/homilies/2013/documents/papa-francesco_20130314_omelia-cardinali.html

contained in our anti-discrimination laws.

The main tension in the community is over religious freedom as expressed through exemptions, but the former Coalition government tried to remedy this tension through a *Religious Discrimination Bill*. The bill, for the most part, was a solution to the wrong problem. It was trying to solve religious discrimination when the real battleground remains religious freedom.

Whatever of the failed attempt, the *Religious Discrimination Bill* did give us some insight of where the future Albanese Labor Government was going to go with religious discrimination laws.

On 9 February this year, in the early evening of the second reading debate over former Prime Minister Scott Morrison's *Religious Discrimination Bill*, then Opposition Leader now Prime Minister Anthony Albanese outlined the four amendments that Labor would seek to move in the House and, if unsuccessful, in the Senate[1]. Each of these gave an indication of Labor's thinking on religious discrimination.

The bill as drafted included a provision that would protect statements of belief made in good faith that were not malicious and would not reasonably be considered to threaten, intimidate, harass or vilify a person or group from being seen as discrimination[2]. To the extent required, the provision would have also overridden any state laws that would try to label such statements as discriminatory. The bill specifically named subsection 17(1) of the Tasmanian *Anti-Discrimination Act 1998* as one of the items of legislation it would override, ensuring what

---

1 Commonwealth, Parliamentary Debates, House of Representatives, 9 February 2022.. Available at: https://parlinfo.aph.gov.au/parlInfo/search/display/display.w3p;query=Id%3A%22chamber%2Fhansardr%2F25465%2F0187%22

2 *Religious Discrimination Bill 2022*, s12.

happened to Archbishop Julian Porteous did not occur again.

Amendments moved by Labor sought to remove the state override, meaning that non-vilifying statements of belief made in good faith could still be treated as discrimination[1].

Separately to this, the second amendment moved by Labor was to include anti-vilification provisions within the *Religious Discrimination Bill*[2], a process that most faith groups agreed could be kept separate.

The third amendment was to extend existing obligations placed on religious aged care facilities to those religious groups providing aged care at a person's home[3].

And finally, Labor indicated it would move a wholesale repeal of section 38(3) of the *Sex Discrimination Act*, which is the existing exemption that allows religious schools to discriminate against current and prospective students on the basis of sexual orientation and gender identity[4]. This same amendment was moved by Centre Alliance MP Rebekah Sharkie and ended up being passed by the House. I will discuss the effect of the removal of this exemption on religious schools in a moment, but for now, it is worth mentioning that this amendment was significant for another reason as well.

Despite repeated assurances to religious leaders from then

1 The Parliament of the Commonwealth of Australia. Amendments to Government Amendments [Sheet PX133]. Available at: https://parlinfo.aph.gov.au/parlInfo/download/legislation/amend/r6821_amend_c70e5077-0e43-462b-a532-fc0a755ea7fc/upload_pdf/22169%20Dreyfus_2.pdf;fileType=application%2Fpdf

2 The Parliament of the Commonwealth of Australia. Amendments to Government Amendments [Sheet PX133]. Available at: https://parlinfo.aph.gov.au/parlInfo/download/legislation/amend/r6821_amend_31568dc0-a744-4ca5-aeb1-faed9126d411/upload_pdf/22169%20Dreyfus_1.pdf;fileType=application%2Fpdf

3 Ibid.
4 Ibid.

Prime Minister Scott Morrison and then Attorney-General Michaelia Cash that no deal had been done on the removal of exemptions, Mr Albanese tabled a letter he received from the Prime Minister three months earlier, on 1 December 2021, saying that the Government would move its own amendment to repeal section 38(3) in order to get the bill across the line.

We can take from this, I would suggest, that it is only a matter of time before religious schools lose this exemption for good.

I would also like to outline the promises that Labor took to the federal election. There were two ways in which Labor made its position known, first in its 2021 National Platform, and then in response to questions raised by religious groups in advance of the May 2022 poll.

Labor's national platform confirmed that 'Every Australian – no matter their identity, gender, religion, race or sexuality – should be able to live free from discrimination' and committed to protecting and promoting 'the right to freedom of thought, conscience and religion in accordance with Australia's international obligations.' It stated that 'Labor believes in and supports the right of all Australians to have and to manifest their religion or beliefs, and the right of religious organisations to act in accordance with the doctrines, tenets, beliefs or teachings of their faith. Such rights should be protected by law and, in accordance with Article 18 of the International Covenant on Civil and Political Rights, subject only to such limitations as are necessary to protect public safety, order, health, or morals or the fundamental rights and freedoms of others.'[1]

The national platform did not promise a religious discrimination bill, but rather foreshadowed a consolidation of federal

1   Australian Labor Party. National Platform: As adompted at the 2021 Special Platform Conference. March 2021. Available at: https://alp.org.au/media/2594/2021-alp-national-platform-final-endorsed-platform.pdf

anti-discrimination laws that would 'include a review of existing exemptions to ensure that they do not place Australians in a position where they cannot access essential social services.'[1]

That's the real nub of it there: existing exemptions, as I mentioned at the beginning, the legislative means by which we currently exercise our religious freedoms, will be under review.

In its pre-election statements to religious groups[2], Labor committed to acting on protecting Australians against discrimination on religious belief and activity as a priority. It also committed to protecting students in religious schools from discrimination while maintaining the ability of religious schools to teach in accordance with their doctrine, and to protect teachers from discrimination while allowing religious schools to preference people of their own faith in employment.

Given the complexity, Labor has committed to the previous Morrison Government's promise of an Australian Law Reform Commission Review, with one seemingly small but significant change that should concern all religious groups.

In meetings with religious leaders since the Labor Government was elected, Attorney-General Mark Dreyfus has indicated that his office will work on a religious discrimination bill this year with a view to introducing it next year, using the version that passed the House of Representatives – notably with the removal of the section 38(3) exemption – as the starting point for a new bill.

Before progressing the bill, however, the Government will focus on a federal independent commission against corruption and conclude the Australian Law Reform Commission inquiry into the removal of exemptions.

Let's not understate the importance of this. The 'existing'

1 Ibid.
2 https://www.religiousdiscriminationsurvey.au/

bill, for want of a better term, with the exemption allowing religious schools to discriminate on the basis of sexual orientation or gender identity already repealed, will be the starting point. But even before this bill gets tabled, the law reform commission inquiry, tasked with inquiring into the removal or limitation of other existing religious exemptions, will complete its work.

The former Morrison government had set the passage of its *Religious Discrimination Bill* as a pre-condition to the law reform commission inquiry, so that the exemptions would not be removed or limited without a religious discrimination bill being in place.

The reversal of this process means that religious groups could find their existing exemptions, their means by which they exercise religious freedom, restricted or removed altogether before any religious discrimination bill is passed.

WILL A RELIGIOUS DISCRIMINATION BILL PASS?

The big issue with all of this is that I believe it is unlikely, perhaps even impossible, that a religious discrimination bill that provides any meaningful protection for individuals or institutions of faith will pass at all.

We know that the Greens will oppose any legislation that offers robust protection for religious expression, which means that the only option is for a bipartisan approach to getting the bill through the Senate.

This might be possible, particularly given the Coalition Opposition tends to lean more favourably to religious concerns, but we need to remember that Labor requires the support of the Greens during this term to get any of its other legislation through the Senate.

I am not confident, and I don't believe you should be either, that Labor will risk its relationship with the Greens and its broader legislative agenda to appease religious groups. If the public campaigning that occurred earlier this year is anything to go by, there will certainly be no votes in it and the recent census results showing a decline in religious affiliation and a significant increase of those identifying as having no religion, we cannot expect this to be a hill upon which Labor is willing to die.

What happens if we get the Australian Law Reform Commission inquiry with no religious discrimination bill?

I would suggest that the most likely outcome for religious groups is that the Australian Law Reform Commission inquiry into removing or restricting religious exemptions, particularly those exemptions in the *Sex Discrimination Act* that deal with sexual orientation and gender identity, will proceed and that legislation will be introduced to limit those rights. A process for a religious discrimination bill will then get underway but without bearing much fruit, and so we will be left in a position where existing freedoms have been whittled away and no one with the political desire or clout to rectify that mess.

How might such a legislative environment affect the way we operate our institutions?

RELIGIOUS SCHOOLS

The starting point for any religious discrimination bill will be the repeal of section 38(3) of the *Sex Discrimination Act*, that is if the law reform commission inquiry doesn't get to it first.

No one likes the idea of discriminating against students and we have heard from many well-meaning, but might I suggest, misguided school and religious leaders that we do not use or want these exemptions.

But this isn't about treating students who experience same-sex attraction or gender dysphoria badly. It is about maintaining a religious environment in our schools.

Religious schools are small religious communities, and

these exemptions are important to ensuring a religious culture. Let's look at a couple of examples.

Removal of the ability to discriminate against students on the basis of sexual orientation or gender identity will affect the way religious schools are able to teach about marriage and family, sexual and reproductive ethics.

Repeal of the exemption in relation to students could result in an obligation for schools offering sex education to treat all types of sexual activity equally.

Anti-discrimination law prohibits the denial of a benefit to a person on the basis of a protected attribute, including sexual orientation. If an anti-discrimination tribunal considers the provision of relevant sex education to be a 'benefit,' then a religious school would have to offer education on all forms of sexual activity on the same terms.

Going further, Catholic teaching opposing IVF and surrogacy could also be viewed as discrimination against 'rainbow families.' If Australia follows Canada's lead, it could even be that parents would not be able to remove their children from any such classes, because having students leave before same-sex sex education was offered could be labelled as bullying. This was the basis of the Safe Schools program, if you recall. That was not a sex education program, but rather an anti-bullying one.

It not only affects what a child learns at school, but also what they are taught at home.

Suppose a child at a religious primary school is experiencing gender dysphoria and decides to socially transition at school. The removal of section 38(3) of the *Sex Discrimination Act* prevents any form of discrimination against a student on the basis of their gender identity, so the school will have to allow this transition and everything that comes with it: school uniform, use of facilities, sporting teams, camp accommodation and more, and parents of other students will not be able to object.

That much is a given.

But what about name and pronoun use?

A child who socially transitions will likely present at school wanting to use a different name and gender pronoun. Imagine your child or grandchild comes home from school and asks about the change and how they should refer to their new classmate.

Anything but affirmation could be seen as a form of discrimination and could land the school in trouble under the *Sex Discrimination Act* if a student or teacher who refuses the change in name and pronoun is not disciplined.

Moreover, without an override of state-based anti-discrimination laws, genuine statements of religious belief would also not be protected from state-based anti-discrimination complaints, leaving an individual susceptible to making such a claim.

All this is by way of saying that not only will parents who choose a religious education for their children no longer be able to count on the school being able to partner with them as teachers in the faith, the school will ultimately be legally required to undermine the efforts being made at home as well.

And this is before we even get to matters of staffing, which is the next item on the list.

As mentioned previously, Labor's election promise was to prevent discrimination against teachers while simultaneously allowing religious schools to preference teachers who share their faith.

What this means practically is that the only grounds on which a school may discriminate against an existing or potential employee will be religious belief or activity. Other attributes, such as marital status or gender identity, will not be captured.

A school wanting to ensure that its teaching staff publicly

abide by the sexual ethics of the faith of the school will need to argue that a person who does not adhere to such teachings place themselves outside the bounds of a member of that religion. This is a tough argument to make at the best of times, but is made more difficult in several respects: not only the public rejection of Christian sexual ethics by many Christians but also, the number of religious institutions who have failed to discipline such public rejection over the years. As one example, a Catholic girls' school in Sydney had teachers actively encourage students to attend a pro-abortion protest back in 2019[1], and even attended alongside them. These teachers were not disciplined, to my knowledge. Given this, it would be difficult for that same school to then seek to reject an application from a transgender teacher, or to discipline an existing teacher who entered into a same-sex marriage, because we will not be allowed to 'pick and choose' the aspects of religious doctrine we decide to enforce amongst staff. Generations of turning a blind eye are about to reap devastating rewards on all our institutions, not just our schools.

This isn't necessarily about trying to keep everyone whose life doesn't reflect the teachings of the faith out of a job in religious institutions. We are all sinners, after all. However, these exemptions allow us to keep activists out of our schools and institutions. I have had first-hand experience of a transgender activist gaining employment in one of our organisations, only to reveal their trans identity the day after their probation period ended. Religious institutions need exemptions not to keep well-meaning people out, they need them to protect against activists.

1   Rushton G. This Catholic Schoolgirl Made An Abortion Rights March Event And It Blew Up To Thousands Of People. BuzzFeed News. 4 June 2019. Available at: https://www.buzzfeed.com/ginarushton/reproductive-rights-march-sydney-australia

OTHER INSTITUTIONS

Consider the leadership of health and social services organisations as well. In the debate over the Morrison *Religious Discrimination Bill*, Catholic welfare agencies such as St Vincent de Paul went so far as to publicly oppose the submission by Catholic Bishops asking for institutional protections[1]. Again, to my knowledge, not a single person was disciplined over this and each of the Society's most senior members at the time are still in their roles.

If I move beyond the removal of federal exemptions for just a moment, we might also predict that similar events will happen when it comes to state-based anti-discrimination laws, particularly now that there is no threat of a federal override.

Victoria has already severely limited religious exemptions and a number of others, including Tasmania, are poised to do the same. Even in New South Wales, Independent MP Alex Greenwich, who has managed to usher in abortion and euthanasia laws in a single term of parliament under the country's only remaining so-called conservative government is now consulting about an omnibus equality bill that will do everything from ban so-called conversion therapy to remove religious exemptions in anti-discrimination law.

We can be quite certain that a federal Labor government that in opposition was already rejecting an override of state anti-discrimination laws will have no interest in holding their state Labor counterparts to account.

The most egregious example of this might be seen in the Australian Capital Territory. A bill released for consultation

---

1   St Vincent de Paul Society National Council of Australia Inc. Statement to Society Members, Companions, Volunteers, Employees & Supporters: Religious Discrimination Bill. 19 January 2022. Available at: https://www.vinnies.org.au/icms_docs/329732_STATEMENT_-_Religious_Discrimination_Bill.pdf

that will likely pass in the coming months will see anti-discrimination law amended in such a way as to see the government not only intrude on employment matters, but also on liturgical ones[1].

A government-issued fact sheet accompanying the draft bill[2] indicated that anti-discrimination laws would intervene into matters such as worship, admission to the sacraments and even ordination. I can't be certain, but I believe that the intrusion of a government into the liturgical and sacramental life of a church is unprecedented outside of China but still, no warning from the federal government that attempts to do so will be reined in.

I would like to conclude this paper on a practical and possibly even hopeful note by offering five ways that we might consider taking action, individually and collectively.

1. Refuse to participate in the ALRC process

My first suggestion is that we seriously need to consider, as religious bodies, refusing to participate in any Australian Law Reform Commission inquiry that precedes the passage of a meaningful religious discrimination bill. As much as we have to contribute to this process, by participating in it without being certain of any protections on the other side, we give it credence.

---

1 Minister for Human Rights. Exposure Draft: Discrimination Amendment Bill 2022 (ACT). Available at: https://hdp-au-prod-app-act-yoursay-files.s3.ap-southeast-2.amazonaws.com/5916/5405/1134/J2022-244-Discrimination_Amendment_Bill_2022-D06_Final.PDF

2 ACT Government. Public Exposure Draft: Discrimination Amendment Bill 2022. Available at: https://hdp-au-prod-app-act-yoursay-files.s3.ap-southeast-2.amazonaws.com/5616/5413/0668/Fact_Sheet_-_Exposure_Draft_Discrimination_Amendment_Bill_2022.pdf

It is a conversation for faith leaders and political operatives smarter than I, but we should at least acknowledge that one card we have to play is that we can delegitimise this process by sitting it out. We don't have to play the hand that we are dealt every time.

2. Collect data

The next thing we need to do is to collect data on religious discrimination in this country, particularly discrimination experienced by Christians. Our Islamic and Jewish brothers and sisters are very good at reporting on and responding to incidents of Islamophobia and anti-Semitism respectively, but Christians as a whole do not do this well, and struggle to combat the narrative that religious discrimination against Christians does not exist in this country. If we joined together to collect and publish reliable data, it would be much more difficult for incidents of discrimination to be dismissed.

3. Community life

If my predictions are correct, and our schools and health and welfare providers become more like NGOs and indeed, more like government agencies than religious institutions, then we need to find other ways of supporting families seeking to raise their children in faith and sustaining religious community life.

Instead of relying on schools to be small communities of faith, we will need to rebuild these communities in our parishes. We need to be intentional about having families of faith come together to support each other and to provide their children with friends who are being raised by those who share the same beliefs.

We can be creative, doing things like having parishes offer school holiday programs that unashamedly offer catechesis so that children will be educated in the faith while having the practical benefit of providing a solution for parents looking for inexpensive school holiday activities.

4. Exercising our religious freedoms now

The other, practical idea is that we need to continue to exercise our religious freedoms, proclaiming Christ and the truth of our faith boldly. As I mentioned before, the refusal to discipline public rejection of religious belief by those who are employed in our institutions has been a body blow to our present ability to defend our religious freedom. The best way to protect our freedoms is to use them boldly and unashamedly now, and support others who do the same.

There is no reason at all for a Christian school that comes under attack for asking teachers to sign a statement of faith, or for publishing a policy on how it will deal with a transgender student, to be fighting alone.

It was actually Lyle Shelton, who said to me in relation to the Archbishop Porteous case that we should never allow one of our brethren to be out on the battlefield alone.

5. Prayer

And finally, we need to pray. We believe that prayer is efficacious and that God does indeed hear our cries. Indeed, in times like this, there is nothing more practical than prayer because it is not just earthly governments we fight, but powers and principalities as well.

On that note, I will conclude this paper in prayer.

Father, we praise you and thank you for your most precious gifts of human life and human freedom. You have called us as your people and given us the right and the duty to worship you, the only true God, and your Son, Jesus Christ. Through the power and working of your Holy Spirit, you call us to live out our faith in the midst of the world, bringing the light and the saving truth of the Gospel to every corner of society. We ask you to bless us in our vigilance for the gift of religious freedom. Give us the strength of mind and heart to readily defend our freedoms when they are threatened; courage in making our voices heard on behalf of all people of faith and a clear and united voice so that, with every trial withstood and every danger overcome— for the sake of all who come after us— this fair land will always be 'young and free.' Amen.

CHRISTIANITY AND FREE EXPRESSION: AN UNEASY HISTORICAL RELATIONSHIP

Lucas McLennan

ABSTRACT

In this paper, I will explore how Christian societies in ancient, medieval, and early modern periods did not share modern enlightenment-based ideals of free speech and expression. I will argue that Christian communities today, while very much in need of a culture that respects freedom of speech and expression, should still ultimately recognise that their cause is truth. The principle of free expression should not be an ultimate ideal of its own.

INTRODUCTION: BEFORE CONSTANTINE

In 157 AD, St. Justin Martyr addressed the Roman Senate and defended Rome's Christians against the propaganda that had led to their persecution. The Martyr accuses Urbicus of lying about the early Church. They had been called 'atheist' and 'impious.'[1] by the authorities. St. Justin goes to some length to explain why that was not the case. Christians, he believed, show the seriousness of their belief by willingly going to their deaths.[2] The Roman Empire, like all great em-

---

[1] 'The Second Apology of Justin Martyr,' Fordham University, accessed 20 June, 2022, https://sourcebooks.fordham.edu/basis/justin-apology2.asp

[2] 'Second Apology.'

pires of the past, had a religious cult. Nevertheless, the Roman Empire could provide a great degree of toleration for its subject peoples, provided that the emperor was acknowledged as divine. Jews and Christians, therefore, struggled to fit into an otherwise tolerant empire.

What Justin Martyr does not argue in his second Apology is the concept that Christians should simply be free to believe and practice their religion without interference. He instead claims that what Christians believe in is the truth. Therefore, they should not be condemned to death or persecuted because it is the truth. So, while Rome was known for having a generally free attitude to religious beliefs, Justin Martyr does not use this fact in his Apology. He instead argues that Christians have been lied about unfairly and that their beliefs are justifiable.[1]

Today, many Christians (and other religious believers) make recourse to the principle of free speech and expression when defending their right to speak on contentious moral issues. Of course, there is nothing wrong with that at all. However, this paper will seek to describe and narrate the uneasy relationship between the Christian religion and free speech and expression. I will begin by outlining the relationship between Church and State in the western world through three periods.[2] The first period of Christendom (approx. 313-1517—the Reformation), the second period of the confessional state (approx. 1555-1789—the French Revolution), and finally, the age of revolution, where in many countries, the link between church and state was ended or at least heavily eroded.[3] In all these periods, the fused church

    1   'Second Apology.'
    2   My focus is on Western Europe and the societies that emerged from the expansion of those societies.
    3   Hilary Carey and John Gascoigne, 'Introduction: The Rise and Fall of Christendom,' in *Church and State in Old and New Worlds*, ed. Hilary Carey and John Gascoigne (Leiden: Brill, 2010), 1-27. The introduction

and state lacked a commitment to free speech and expression according to the modern liberal understanding. In the age of revolution, European church opponents used conceptions of free speech and expression to remove their power and unique status in the social order. As a result, the churches and the liberal revolutionary movements often were against one another.

The liberal regimes that emerged in Europe and the wider western world were often built on a continuing Christian moral and social culture. As a result, many dissenting protestants (Catholics in the Anglo countries) benefited from the emerging liberal and secular order. In the last few decades, however, liberal secular society has primarily lost its underlying Christian culture. As a result, a secular progressive worldview often frames religious beliefs as 'unsafe' and dangerous. In response, Christians resort to the claim that the public square should be neutral.

I sincerely hope that this contribution to the Dawson Colloquium draws participants attention to the complex history of the relationship between the Christian religion and free speech and expression.

CHRISTENDOM

The conversion of the Roman Emperor Constantine began a gradual process where the Church was tolerated, promoted, and then established as the only Imperial religion. In his adopted role as protector of the Church, Constantine used his power to ensure that theological divisions in the Church were resolved.

Despite his Arian leanings, the First Council of Nicaea defined the doctrine of the Holy Trinity. Constantine at first

---

of Carey and Gascoigne is helpful in categorising the timeline of the history of church-state relations. I have drawn of their categorisation of epochs in this paper.

respected this decision. Then, however, he used the power of the Empire to punish those who dissented from the Council's proclamations.[1]

By the time of the collapse of the Roman Empire in the west (generally dated as 476 AD), the Church had been declared the only legal religion or cult in the Empire. The states that would emerge in Western Europe in the coming centuries would all intimately fuse the Church and State. It is probably more helpful to think of the situation as a fusion between Church and crown or sovereign.

Under Emperor Charlemagne, the Church and Empire were deeply linked. Even with the division of his territories after his death, the Church emerged as the only European-wide institution. Amongst the squabbling of Emperors and princes, the era between Charlemagne and the Reformation can rightly be called Christendom. Essentially all people were members of the Church, and the culture of the Church provided a common understanding between the otherwise warring princes of Europe. It was truly one civilisation. At the same time, there were occasional dissenters like the Hussites. There was also an ever-present Jewish minority. However, full participation in civic life assumed that one was sacramentally a member of the Church. The Church functioned as a United Nations or EU-like institution. It was supranational in its nature and practices. While it is confusing for those who think of the modern nation-state, Christendom was a single civilisation and system.

In no sense was there clear freedom to dissent from the teachings of the Church. However, in his defence of Christianity and the west, Rodney Stark has argued that the medieval European universities fostered a spirit of inquiry and critical

---

1   Joseph Kelly, *The Ecumenical Councils of the Catholic Church* (Collegeville, MN: Liturgical Press), 21-29.

thinking. Stark contrasts this open spirit with the rigid Confucian system of Chinese civilisation, where you had to master the ideas of Confucius. You had to propose a new argument in medieval Europe in your research.[1] But the medieval universities still had broad parameters, and one could hear no dissent from the defined teachings of the Church. There was no general religious freedom and no recognised right to freedom of speech. On the contrary, obedience to the Church was necessary for the salvation of souls and social order.

The case of the Hussites is the most appropriate example. Czech priest Jan Hus (ca. 1372-1415) adopted the ideas of English reformer John Wycliffe. He believed that clergy that were corrupt or immoral lost their legitimacy. Operating at a time in which there were rival papacies in the Catholic Church, Hus was condemned and excommunicated by two papal claimants.[2] He took refuge in Bohemia (the Czech lands). Hus requested a hearing at the Council of Constance. Whilst traveling there, he was arrested. The Council found him guilty of heresy, and was executed in 1415. In later years he would inspire a rebellion in the Czech lands.[3]

There are two essential things to note here. Firstly, it was the Church that tried and punished Jan Hus. Throughout the Middle Ages, the Church was recognised with the competency to convict and punish canonical crimes like heresy. Throughout Christendom, the Princes were responsible for the enforcement of their civic sphere, and the Church was left to enforce laws in its sphere. The Church was, therefore, the guardian of what could be expressed in the public square, in universities, and in other places where people gathered in society. Consequently,

[1] Rodney Stark, *How the West was Won* (Wilmington: ISI Books), 151-189.
[2] Kelly, 112, Op. cit.
[3] Ibid.

we can see that during the era of Christendom, the Church did not accept an uninhibited right to free expression and speech in the social order.

THE CONFESSIONAL STATE

The culture of the Middle Ages saw a profound union of culture, language, and belief, all under the authority of the Church. However, this continent-wide Christian culture fractured under the pressure of the Reformation. Rather than having a European-wide cultural order, each European state that adopted the principles of one of the Reformation strands created its own fused Church-State. This can be described as the era of the confessional state. In places like England and Scandinavia, the new state churches were very much under the authority of the state. Only in Catholic states did some semblance of the old understanding of Christendom remain. But even in those countries, the principle of *cuius regio, eius religio* (whose region, his religion) (first established at the Peace of Augsburg in 1555) meant an awareness of the instability of religious belief became clear. If the prince could choose his religious affiliation, why could this not also be extended to his subjects? Questions emerged as to how populations who dissented from the choices of their prince should be dealt with. Forms of religious toleration were tried with varying success in England, France, and Prussia.

John Calvin's Geneva is a helpful example to explore in the confessional state period. Due to Calvinism's influence on the British settlement of North America and in the short-lived Commonwealth of Cromwell, Calvin's ideas have been identified as proto-democratic.[1] There is significant weight in

---

1   Mervyn Davies, *Foundations of American Freedom: Calvinism in the Development of Democracy* (Nashville: Abingdon).

these interpretations because of the presbyterian governance structure of the Calvinist churches. Whilst forms of democracy can be attributed to Calvin's branch of Protestantism, ideals of freedom of speech, expression, and a neutral public space cannot be. Calvin spent the last two decades of his life in Geneva, where he was given the responsibility of drafting and implementing a constitution for a new church-state relationship that fused religion and the state and placed limits on the free expression of opinion.

More so than in the Lutheran states of Europe, Calvin insisted upon the spiritual independence of the Church. In Book 4 of his *Institutes of the Christian Religion*, he states:

> *The Church is regarded in two points of view; as Invisible and Universal, which is the communion of saints; and as Visible and Particular. The Church is discerned by the pure preaching of the word, and by the lawful administration of the sacraments.*[1]

In Calvin's understanding, the catholic church existed worldwide as a spiritual communion of believers. The roman papacy had corrupted its visible form. Communities that adopted his principles of the Reformation (preaching the Word and his understanding of the sacraments) could form valid local and 'visible' churches. Such churches did not need to be independent of the state. The Council of Geneva voted to adopt the reformation principles of Calvin, and he saw ecclesial and civil governments as linked. His Institutes state, 'God keeps us united in the fellowship of Christ by means of

---

1   'Calvin's Institutes of the Christian Religion aphorisms,' Christian Classics Ethereal Library, accessed 31 May, 2022, https://www.ccel.org/ccel/calvin/institutes.vii.iv.html.

Ecclesiastical and Civil government.'[1] This demonstrates that Calvin recognised that (where feasible) the civil magistrate could play a role in overseeing the Church. In Calvin's vision, the civil ruler was the 'father of his country, the guardian of the laws, the administrator of justice, the defender of the Church.'[2] Consequently, a state that adopted the independent church model of the Reformation imposed on its ruler a direct role in the governance and protection of the state Church.

In Calvin's Geneva, the civil government was utilised to impose religious and ideological uniformity on the population. The infamous case of Jerome Bolsec (a French theologian) is a case in point. He was banished from Geneva for heresy in 1551. His thought crime was that he had publicly challenged Calvin's doctrine of predestination. Another example is the execution of Michael Servetus in 1553 for denying the Trinity.

Whilst these are extreme examples and very rare, they all provide concrete examples of Calvin's understanding that the state should recognise the church and play a role in enforcing its theology. The idea of executing or banishing dissidents due to theological disagreements would be abhorrent to almost all modern Christians of whatever stripe. What is very clear, though, is that in both the age of Christendom and the confessional state, the civil order was understood to play a role in regulating the public expression of religious opinion in the public square.[3]

As the age of the Reformation segued into the age of revolutions, the question of church-state relations became paramount. Great Britain established a limited degree of toleration with the Glorious Revolution of 1689. However, the toleration

1 'Calvin's Institutes of the Christian Religion aphorisms.'
2 'Calvin's Institutes of the Christian Religion aphorisms.'
3 Jeffrey R. Watt, *The Consistory and social discipline in Calvin's Geneva* (Rochester: University of Rochester Press), 40-42.

did not extend to Catholics. Many of the state's key institutions remained limited to members of the established Anglican Church. Some examples include the Parliament and the Universities of Oxford and Cambridge. Consequently, dissenting Christian minorities were accepted, but they had to choose to remain outside the social order of the kingdom.

During the confessional state era, France even moved to limit toleration. The French had accepted the presence of the Huguenot minority to bring an end to the Wars of Religion. Under Louis XIV, however, the tolerant Edict of Nantes was revoked, and there was an exodus of Huguenots to the protestant states of Europe.

THE AGE OF REVOLUTIONS

The consequence of the French Revolution was to undermine all features of the old regime in Europe. Rejection of a Church establishment and the ideal of religious freedom and expression emerged as critical principles. In the Declaration of the Rights of Man and Citizen, the members of the revolutionary National Assembly proclaimed, 'The aim of all political association is the preservation of the natural and imprescriptible rights of man. These rights are liberty, property, security, and resistance to oppression.'[1] In Christendom and the confessional states, the state was understood to have a religious as well as materialistic purpose.

Later in the declaration, the right to hold and express one's religious opinions was explicitly recognised:

> *10. No one shall be disquieted on account of his opinions, including his religious views, provided their manifestation does*

[1] 'Declaration of the Rights of Man and Citizen,' Yale Law School, accessed 25 June, 2022, https://avalon.law.yale.edu/18th_century/rightsof.asp.

not disturb the public order established by law.

11. The free communication of ideas and opinions is one of the most precious of the rights of man. Every citizen may, accordingly, speak, write, and print with freedom, but shall be responsible for such abuses of this freedom as shall be defined by law.[1]

The principle of having one formal religion or church was completely under threat. In France, one could now write publicly denouncing the doctrines of the Catholic Church, promote atheism or criticise the rulers without fear unless the public order was endangered (and we know that France fell into tyranny and lawlessness at different points in the following century).

While established churches would be maintained in most European states in the following nineteenth century, often their establishment was understood in purely utilitarian terms. An official religion helped promote the common good. Such a conception was particularly prominent in Britain and its colonies, where the Georgian Bishop William Warburton had articulated that the primary purpose of having a religious establishment was to promote morality and maintain social order.[2]

Protestants and Catholics needed to respond to the revolutionary movement against the tradition of Church-State relations; for the most part, they were hostile to the new developments. Some moderns may think, 'why?' Surely the Christian religion can stand on its own two feet? Perhaps it was better for the Church to be free from state influence? One school of thought, best represented by Alexis de Tocqueville, saw a liberal

1 'Declaration of the Rights of Man and Citizen.'
2 Stephen Taylor, 'William Warburton and the Alliance of Church and State,' *Journal of Ecclesiastical History* 43, Issue 2, (April 1992): 271-286.

society as requiring a pre-existing moral and religious culture.[1] Such an approach is known as 'conservative liberalism.'[2] Indeed, many dissenting protestant confessions like the Baptists, Congregationalists, and others welcomed the coming of liberalism. In the English-speaking world, long dominated by the Anglican establishment, mainly Irish Catholics embraced the ideal of a 'free church in a free state.'[3] For the most part, however, the Catholic Church and the protestant churches of northern Europe adopted a hostile posture towards the new ways of the age of revolutions.

THE REACTION OF THE CATHOLIC CHURCH

In the Catholic countries of Europe (and in their former colonial possessions), the Church encountered a liberal revolutionary spirit that undermined its ability to function. The nineteenth century was a period of revolution and counter-revolution. In Catholic countries, there was no real dispute as to which side the Church sat. It stood opposed to the principles of 1789.

Whenever liberal regimes came to power, they always sought to remove the Church's lands and destroy its role in education. In revolutionary France, the religious orders were banned from education. The revolutionaries knew that a state system of education, free from Church influence, would be necessary if the ideals of 1789 were to survive.

Napoleon normalised relations with the Church in the Concordat of 1801. However, this document represented a significant shift in church-state relations. The concordat rec-

---

1 Daniel J. Mahoney, *The Conservative Foundations of the Liberal Order* (Wilmington: ISI Books, 2010), 2-3.
2 Ibid.
3 Ernst C. Helmreich, 'Introduction,' in *A Free Church in a Free State? The Catholic Church, Italy, Germany, France, 1864-1914*, ed. Ernst C. Helmreich (London: Heath, 1964), 10-20.

ognised a unique role for the Catholic Church only because it was the religion of the 'great majority'[1] of the population. The arrangement was purely practical. Napoleon did not recognise his power as relying on the authority of religion. In the previous era of the confessional states, all monarchs in Europe (Catholic or protestant) would have regarded the protection and promotion of religion as a part of their core mission.

In states like Austria (under Emperor Joseph II and in independent Mexico in their 1857 republican constitution), the Church estates were removed and sold to either private interests or used for state purposes. In both cases, attempts were made to establish a public and secular basis for education.

Surrounded by a hostile ideological climate, the Popes of the nineteenth century firmly expressed the traditional understanding of the unique role of the Catholic Church in traditionally Catholic states. Pope Pius IX most famously did this when he published his Syllabus of Errors in 1864. The syllabus was a collection of statements criticising the modern world of the prior 18 years of Pius IX's papacy.

Pius IX argued that it was an error to think, 'Every man is free to embrace and profess that religion which, guided by the light of reason, he shall consider true.'[2] In this, he lambasted the liberal regimes of Europe and the Catholic thinkers who had advocated the positives of liberal regimes for the Church for Catholics in countries where they did not constitute a majority of the population.

The Pope went on to state that it was unacceptable for Catholics to accept a system of education disconnected

---

1 'Concordat of 1801,' Waterloo Association, accessed 1 July, 2022, https://www.napoleon-series.org/research/government/diplomatic/c_concordat.html.

2 Pius IX, *Syllabus of Errors*, appendix to Encyclical (1864), n. 15.

from Church control.[1] Therefore highlighting that secular or non-sectarian education could never be truly neutral. If religion is not present in an integrated way or presented as a purely private or individual matter, students will learn the lesson that religion is not something essential to their lives and society. Therefore, education can never be described as 'neutral' towards religion.

Finally, Pius IX directly condemns the core problems of modern liberalism. It is worth listing his three errors in full:

> 77. *In the present day it is no longer expedient that the Catholic religion should be held as the only religion of the State, to the exclusion of all other forms of worship.* — Allocution 'Nemo vestrum,' July 26, 1855.
>
> 78. *Hence it has been wisely decided by law, in some Catholic countries, that persons coming to reside therein shall enjoy the public exercise of their own peculiar worship.* — Allocution 'Acerbissimum,' Sept. 27, 1852.
>
> 79. *Moreover, it is false that the civil liberty of every form of worship, and the full power, given to all, of overtly and publicly manifesting any opinions whatsoever and thoughts, conduce more easily to corrupt the morals and minds of the people, and to propagate the pest of indifferentism.* — Allocution 'Nunquam fore,' Dec. 15, 1856 [2]

To phrase these as positive statements we would say:

1. It is fitting that the Catholic religion should be recognised as the religion of the state.

2. Non-Catholic religions do not enjoy an unlimited right to worship and practice their own religion freely in Catholic states.

---

[1] Pius IX, *Syllabus of Errors*, n. 48.
[2] Pius IX, *Syllabus of Errors*, n. 78-79.

3. Freedom of religion inevitably leads to an attitude that all religions are essentially the same, creating a view that is indifferent to the ultimate truth.

While there were many Catholics who felt uncomfortable with the way these ideals were expressed in the syllabus, what is clear is that the Church, having encountered the concepts of modern liberalism, firmly rejected them and sought *at least in Catholic countries) to hold onto its privileged position as the arbiter of religious truth and practice.

Despite adopting such a strong line of defence against modern liberalism and strengthening this line of defence at the First Vatican Council (1870), the next century would see the adoption of liberalism in some form in all the Catholic countries of Europe. The Church may have been right in expressing these ideals, but it was unsuccessful in having them persevered in any Catholic country.

CONCLUSION

How are we to respond to this history?

First, we must recognise that the free exploration of ideas is important. Christians in previous centuries rightly sought to preserve the Church's role in the European countries' public life. In failing in such efforts, we must also recognise that the liberal concept of a 'neutral public square' is not genuinely possible.

We can argue for the right to free expression, but secular progressives will ultimately see this as dangerous.

We need to fight for the right of church communities to form their own communities that adhere to a Christ-centric vision of the good.

Ultimately, we need to understand that concepts of a secular state and the neutral public square cannot hide the reality that the state is never neutral on a vision for the common good.

In this presentation, I have outlined various episodes from the history of Western Christianity. These episodes show how powers aligned with the churches were not customarily disposed to an unlimited free expression of ideas and debate. Thinkers like Pope Benedict XVI have often linked the development of the Enlightenment with the Christian understanding of human dignity. However, the drive to separate church and state and establish liberal freedoms in the age of revolutions was met with hostility by the Catholic Church and the protestant state churches of northern Europe.

I draw attention to these episodes because modern western Christians are often surprised when secular progressives do not live up to their pluralism and free speech principles. We need to understand that secular progressive movements have a vision of the common good that is at odds with a traditional Christian vision. As a result, a conflict emerges, and only one vision of the common good can have the endorsement of the state. Any other situation is schizophrenic. It is beyond the scope of this presentation to explore the 'falsity' of liberal claims about free expression, pluralism, and the neutral public square, but fortunately, there are a range of thinkers working on the topic currently.[1]

Finally, thank you for accepting this piece of historical exploration within this broader discussion on the relationship between Christianity and free speech.

---

[1] Patrick Deneen's work *Why Liberalism Failed* (Yale: Yale University Press, 2018) is a particularly good example.

THE TWO WINGS – FAITH AND REASON
Archbishop Julian Porteous

ABSTRACT

The intellectual tradition in Western civilisation has been grounded in the interplay of faith and reason. The faith is the Christian faith which shaped Western civilisation for a millennium. Reason draws on the development of philosophical thought, tracing itself back to the pre-Christian Greek Philosophers. In this paper I will explore the rise of ideology in contemporary society, arguing that it stands in direct opposition to the tradition of the interrelationship between faith and reason which is necessary for the development of culture and healthy patterns of human life. In particular I will give attention to the effect of ideology on freedom of speech in contemporary society.

THE INTELLECTUAL TRADITION in Western civilisation has been grounded in the interplay of faith and reason. The faith here is the Christian faith which has shaped Western culture. Reason draws on the development of philosophical thought, tracing itself back to the pre-Christian Greek Philosophers.

Pope John Paul II began his 1998 encyclical, *Fides et Ratio*, Faith and Reason, declaring: 'Faith and reason are like two wings on which the human spirit rises to the contemplation of truth'.[1] He added, 'God has placed in the human heart a

---

1 Pope John Paul II, *Fides et Ratio*, 1998, no 100, https://www.vatican.va/content/john-paul-ii/en/encyclicals/documents/hf_jp-ii_enc_14091998_fides-et-ratio.html

desire to know the truth'.¹ This is a foundational Christian understanding. St Anselm of Canterbury described theology as *Fides quaerens intellectum*, faith seeking understanding. He commented, 'I do not seek to understand in order that I may believe, but rather, I believe in order that I may understand'². Faith precedes understanding – this is the Christian basis for the pursuit of truth.

The encyclical, *Fides et Ratio*, argues for the importance of the discipline of philosophy not only for the Church but for the flourishing of human culture. St John Paul says,

*The importance of philosophical thought in the development of culture and its influence on patterns of personal and social behaviour is there for all to see. In addition, philosophy exercises a powerful, though not always obvious, influence on theology and its disciplines. For these reasons, I have judged it appropriate and necessary to emphasize the value of philosophy for the understanding of the faith, as well as the limits which philosophy faces when it neglects or rejects the truths of Revelation. The Church remains profoundly convinced that faith and reason mutually support each other.*³

In this paper I would like to explore the rise of ideology in contemporary society, arguing that it stands in direct opposition to the tradition of the interrelationship between faith and reason which Pope St John Paul II sees as necessary for the development of culture and healthy patterns of human life.

PHILOSOPHY AND IDEOLOGY

Philosophy, coming from the Greek words, *philo* and *sophos*, has as its purpose the love of wisdom and the pursuit of truth.

1   Ibid.
2   St. Anselm, *Proslogion*, Chapter 1, https://sourcebooks.fordham.edu/basis/anselm-proslogium.asp#CHAPTER%20I
3   Op.cit. *Fides et Ratio*.

The philosopher looks at reality and seeks to understand it. Philosophy has an attitude of reverence before reality and is open to being shaped by it. Philosophy is a search for the truth of things. Philosophy, while it seeks to understand reality, also recognises humbly that it cannot master all knowledge about reality.

In a talk on 1 April 2005 Cardinal Joseph Ratzinger (later Pope Benedict XVI) emphasised that faith and reason are not incompatible. He argued:

> 'From the beginning, Christianity has understood itself as the religion of the *Logos*, as the religion according to reason'.[1]

Thus, in the mind of Ratzinger, a person of faith has no problem with the use of rational thought. He describes the Logos as 'creative reason', and argues that the Christian is 'open to all that is truly rational'.

By way of contrast, ideology is a closing of the mind around one pre-conceived idea. Ideology arrives at an idea which may be the result of philosophical or scientific enquiry but then seeks to conform everything to this prevailing view of reality. While philosophy will continue its search for truth, ideology will close itself to further questioning and will, in fact, reject anything that does not fit its view of reality.

Philosophy realises that the world is complex and hard to comprehend. Its enquiry seeks to understand while aware of its limits. On the other hand, in the face of the complexity of human reality, ideology develops a theory which explains everything and then barricades itself around this idea.

1 Joseph Cardinal Ratzinger, On Europe's Crisis of Culture, https://www.ewtn.com/catholicism/library/zenit-daily-dispatch-2968

RISE OF IDEOLOGY

We live in an age of ideology. One of the key reasons for the rise of ideology is the demise of religion and cultural patterns shaped by religion that have in the past provided meaning and value to human existence. However, our culture in the West is rapidly abandoning the element of faith as a constitutive element in human thought. Not accepting the contribution that faith can make, reason is left to its own resources.

As our world has become more interconnected, as access to information has become so readily available, so the sheer complexity of the world has caused a heightened sense of uncertainty. This fosters a yearning for some simple all-encompassing idea on which to hang one's world view.

The twentieth century witnessed the rise of two powerful ideologies, Nazism and Communism. Both, as political ideas, have proved to fail while, in the time of their ascendency, brought suffering on millions of people. However, the Marxist ideology which lay at the heart of Communism has morphed into new cultural expressions which at the present time are having a profound impact on Western culture. In particular, it is currently shaping society's view of gender, sexuality and race. This cultural Marxism lies at the heart of the rise of the Woke movement which has captivated not only the young, but even leaders of business and politics. It is driving social change.

The root of the notion of ideology is linked to a nineteenth century group who called themselves the *ideologues*. The movement proposed the 'scientific' study of ideas. As a movement it came and went. However, Karl Marx embraced the term. Marx conducted what he considered a 'scientific' study of human society. His studies led him to the conclusion that human society is essentially grounded in a class struggle. His theory was not just about the struggle between the capitalist and working classes, but became in his eyes an explanation of the whole of human existence revealed throughout human history. In other words, it was a total picture of reality. Thus, he proposed what he believed was a scientifically rational way to address this struggle but proposing a new way to organise human society.

For Karl Marx philosophy was an abstract process, a philosophy of pure ideas. The ideas then drive political action. While true philosophy will explore the human condition, ideology gives direction to a course of social and political action. A vital shift has taken place as the pursuit of truth is replaced by the determination to act. This action is essentially the will to have controlling power. Marxism's understanding of reality is shaped by a rigorous atheistic materialism. Ideology is driven by a determination to change the current social system.

Thus, for example, the distinction between truth and falsehood rests now not on any moral virtue but simply on whether it advances the ideology or not. There is no longer any transcendental reality and so there is no longer a transcendental truth. The idea is now uppermost and replaces the openness of the mind to find personal meaning and purpose.

Marx adopted a revolutionary standpoint. It all about changing the world. Ideology is essentially an abstract thought which considers itself complete within itself and brooks no self-examination. It has to be acted upon. It has to change things which it sees as wrong. Ideology is the logic of an idea that has to be implemented at any cost.

It assumes that its understanding of reality is sufficient to explain everything and therefore it must be realised. Its source of validation and power is the logical consistency of the idea and does not require an external validation from experience. Indeed, ideology lives to change reality to conform with its driving idea.

One result of this is the will to power so that society can be changed. Human freedom, even among those embracing the ideology, is denied. The idea is everything.

Thus, ideology is based on a single preconception. For Marx it was that history is to be understood as a class struggle. For feminists it is that women's problems are the result of patriarchy. For those who determine that society is plagued by racism it is due to white supremacy. For those who feel alienated, it is the ruling class of white males. It reduces complexity to simple formulas. The ideological thinker organises all reality on the basis of some partial truth, which is developed into a universal interpretation of reality.

IDEOLOGY AND FREEDOM OF SPEECH

For a person driven by ideology dialogue is impossible. The ideologue views all who do not share their view of reality as the enemy. They adopt an antagonistic stance. They readily classify people as belonging to certain categories and they view anyone who has a different view than their own as morally inferior. Those of a different view are seen as evil and oppressors. Ideology is by its nature oriented towards violence.

Thus, in recent times, we have encountered 'cancel culture' and 'de-platforming'. During the Marriage Debate, for instance, threats were made against venues that were booked to present the No Position. When a person dares espouse a contrary view they are attacked, ridiculed and howled down. They are not allowed to speak. We have witnessed this especially in the use of social media to, at times, viciously attack someone who dares propose an alternative view. This is a radical intolerance of any idea contrary to their own.

In the light of the rise of ideology we are experiencing a serious challenge to freedom of speech in our country. It also means that the democratic political system which is built around the robust exchange of ideas becomes ossified.

We cannot escape the world of ideology which is now a

powerful force in contemporary Western culture. It is a world that has chosen to relativise truth. And this relativism has become, as Cardinal Ratzinger famously said, a dictatorship. Now it is the individual person's view of reality that is uppermost. Those who have embraced an ideology be it in relation to gender or sexuality or race are now loud in their denunciation of their opponents and determined to reshape society according to their ideology.

They are absolute in their view and determined to impose it on everyone. Thus, in the pursuit of their objectives education is reduced to indoctrination. Society is being shaped by the force of these ideological positions. They have been able to coerce not only governments but also corporations, sporting bodies and the media such that decent men and women who sense that the ideological position is false are kowtowed into submission by the anger and violence of those who hold the ideological view.

RESPONDING TO IDEOLOGY

How can the tenacious grip of ideology be overcome? Immediately one has to say, 'not easily'.

Ultimately, the answer to ideology lies in the orientation of a person towards the Transcendent. Faith takes a person outside themselves. There is Another to whom one looks. Meaning and purpose are found outside a driving idea. They are found in the person of a loving and merciful God. They are experienced in a relationship which is the fruit of faith. They are nourished by the freedom of choosing to live a life oriented to Someone greater than themselves.

Pope Benedict said, 'Being Christian is not the result of an ethical choice or a lofty idea, but the encounter with an event, a person, which gives life a new horizon and a decisive direction'[1]. In our times it will be an encounter with the Transcendent that can free people from the clutch of an idea.

Secondly, ideology will be overcome by people who adhere to the belief that there is truth, objective and enduring truth. While we cannot argue with an ideologue, it is possible to be a humble witness to truth. When we are alert to the dangers of ideological positions of social questions, we take the simple decision to adhere to the pursuit of truth, living by one's personal beliefs and being armed with a good dose of common sense. The humble belief in truth can be disarming to the ideologue.

In the end it is as Jesus taught: 'the truth will set you free'. (Jn 8:32)

In other words, it will be the interplay of faith and reason that will ultimately provide the antidote to ideology.

---

[1] Pope Benedict XVI, *Deus Caritas Est*, 2005, No 1, https://www.vatican.va/content/benedict-xvi/en/encyclicals/documents/hf_ben-xvi_enc_20051225_deus-caritas-est.html

PICKING UP THE TOOLS OF DEMOCRACY
Lyle Shelton

ABSTRACT

Before it is too late, we must exercise our rights as citizens to participate in politics. Silence and inaction are no longer options if we want to keep the freedom to build virtuous faith-filled families and communities into the future. A partisan political movement to carry the truths of our Western inheritance into the public discourse and parliaments is now also a necessary piece on the battlefield for the soul of our civilisation.

THERE IS NO hope for Australia apart from the Way of Jesus of Nazareth. That's why the work the Dawson Centre plays to preserve the Christian religion is vital for the preservation of our nation. That's why it is such a privilege for me to be here today participating in this colloquium.

My topic is 'picking up the tools of democracy – before it is too late'. This of course is in the context of today's theme of preserving freedom of religion and freedom of speech. My topic is inspired by something said to me at a lunch meeting I had in Canberra some years ago with a former leader of the Opposition in the Canadian Parliament.

Preston Manning is considered the 'father of the Conservative Party' in Canada and he served as its leader from 1997-2000. We were discussing the appropriateness of Christian engagement in politics. There are some who say Christians should stay out of politics and concentrate on saving souls, or at least if they do get involved in politics, stick to social justice issues like poverty and refugees and stay silent on cultural/political issues like same-sex marriage. Manning leaned across the table and said to me that Christians should do what every other free citizen is entitled to do and that is pick up the tools of democracy and use them.

Amid the confusion generated by some prominent Christian voices who felt we had lost the culture wars and therefore should stay out of them, this was a crystalising moment for me.

I want to argue three things in this talk.

One, that the 2017 same-sex marriage plebiscite was the seminal moment when we lost freedom of speech and religion in this nation. We are now no longer in a battle to preserve these things, we are in a battle to restore them.

Two, that freedom of speech and religion will not be restored any time soon by Labor, the so-called 'modern Liberals', the Greens or the Teals. The sad news is that the current political settlement between this quad will not allow it.

Three, that if we want to restore freedom of speech and religion we must use the tools of democracy to create a partisan political movement so that these freedoms are on the ballot paper at every election until they are secure.

The increasing illiberalism of our political and cultural elites means we must build this movement before it is too late.

THE LOSS OF FREEDOM OF SPEECH AND RELIGION

There are so many warriors of the 2017 marriage campaign here today. It's like a happy re-union of those who fought the long defeat. His Grace Archbishop Porteous, Alex Sidhu, Monica Doumit, Dr David van Gend all played key roles in that desperate but necessary rear-guard action. By naming names I am sure to miss some; I'm sure there is not a person here today who was not invested in the campaign in some way—volunteering, door knocking, staffing a telephone call centre or donating money. Thank you for what you did.

Monica, David and I found ourselves performing a public role as media spokespeople in the campaign on behalf of the Coalition for Marriage.

In order to get a message across to a population who were ambivalent about, or supportive of, the 'love is love' mantra, we took every opportunity to remind the Australian people that the marriage vote was a referendum on three things:

1. freedom of speech
2. freedom of religion and
3. the rights of parents to protect their children from radical LGBTIQA+ education at school.

At the time 'Australian Marriage Equality' took great exception to us ventilating these concerns saying they had nothing to do with 'marriage equality'.

But the ink was barely dry on the new legislation when Labor's Penny Wong sought to shepherd a bill through the Parliament taking away the rights of religious schools to employ staff who share their parent community's beliefs on marriage. It was only narrowly defeated when the Centre Alliance party in the Senate declined to support it.

Within less than 12 months of same-sex marriage being legislated, the same-sex marriage campaign, morphed into a permanent campaign machine called Equality Australia run by one of the same-sex marriage campaign leaders, Anna Brown.

Just because they won, the activists had no intention of laying down their weapons. Brown organises woke top tier law firms like Clayton Utz to go after Christian schools like Ballarat Christian College simply because the college requires staff to uphold a Christian ethos on marriage. We've seen attacks on Citipointe Christian College, Bundaberg Christian College and Westside Christian College simply because they sought to exercise their pre-same-sex marriage rights when it comes to upholding a

Christian ethos on marriage and the science of gender.

On a personal level, in January 2020 I wrote a blog about a drag queen story time event that had been held at a Brisbane City Council library. After researching the two drag queens reading to children, I wrote that the drag queens were dangerous role models for children. Here's why:

One was crowd-funding to have her breasts removed and the other boasted on his Facebook page about his award from the so-called Adult entertainment industry – an X Award from the porn trade. He also had an obscene image on his Facebook page readily discoverable by any child with a device.

The drag queens sued me in the Queensland Human Rights Commission and the case has now been escalated to the Queensland Civil and Administrative Tribunal. It has cost me more than $100,000 and this was raised through crowd-funding for which I'm very grateful. The drag queens' lawyers at the LGBT Legal Service in South Brisbane receive hundreds of thousands of dollars from the pockets of Queensland taxpayers. My lawyers, the Human Rights Law Alliance, receive no taxpayer money. They are very busy with cases of people being persecuted at work or sued like me because they won't bow to rainbow ideology.

Australia is no longer a country with freedom of speech, religion or association.

As for radical LGBTIQA+ education at schools, there's hardly a school in the country where the children are not subjected to gender fluid ideology, wear it purple days, Pride Month observances etc. In Victoria, it is government policy for teachers to hide from parents a child's decision to transition his or her gender. I kid you not.

Here's what the Victorian Education Department's LGBTIQ Student Support policy, under the heading 'parental consent', says:

> There may be circumstances in which students wish or need to undertake gender transition without the consent of their parent/s (or carer/s), and/or without consulting medical practitioners.
>
> If no agreement can be reached between the student and the parent/s regarding the student's gender identity, or if the parent/s will not consent to the contents of a student support plan, it will be necessary for the school to consider whether the student is a mature minor.

No government should require teachers to hide anything from parents, let alone a decision as potentially life-altering as gender transition. But hey, when we said the same-sex marriage plebiscite was a referendum on freedom of speech, freedom of religion and parents' rights, the Anna Browns of this world scoffed at us. The chilling effects on basic freedoms since the marriage debate are with us daily.

I recently received an email from 'Catherine', a public servant at a government commission. The email signature block helpfully told me that Catherine's pronouns were – you guessed it—'she, her'. Correction, if you guessed it after hearing the name Catherine, you are a bigot. Had Catherine been a so-called 'trans-woman' and I pushed back, I would have risked being dragged before a tribunal for offending someone on the basis of gender identity, which is a protected attribute under anti-discrimination law.

Everyday Australians who know this is nonsense live in fear of being reported by their colleagues at work wearing rainbow lanyards or ending their emails with pronoun directives. I talk to pastors who tell me they self-censor what they say in the pulpit. In post same-sex marriage Australia, people don't feel safe to speak publicly about the time-honoured view of marriage or the scientific view of gender lest they court controversy.

Sure, some of this was happening pre-2017. But it has been turbo-charged since the law changed, as we said it would. It's just happened more quickly than we thought.

NO RESTORATION ANY TIME SOON

In the dying days of the marriage campaign, just weeks ahead of the November 2017 announcement of the result of the Australian Marriage Law Postal Plebiscite, our campaign about freedoms and parents' rights bore some fruit. After interventions by former Prime Minister John Howard and former Deputy Prime Minister John Anderson, the then Prime Minister Malcolm Turnbull announced that he was setting up the Ruddock Commission into religious freedom.

After a long and drawn-out process, during which the chairman of the commission, former Liberal minister Philip Ruddock, bizarrely declared there was no religious freedom problem in Australia, the Ruddock Commission recommended that laws protecting religious freedom be passed.

After further delays due to Covid, a bill was brought before the federal parliament early this year. Equality Australia and the mainstream media characterised the bill as enabling religious schools to expel gay or transgender students, a power not sought or used by Christian schools. But that didn't matter to the rainbow lobby or the media. Nor did it matter to them that Labor introduced such powers as part of its amendment to the Sex Discrimination Act in 2013.

The die was cast and a lethal narrative set.

Labor, the Greens and the so-called 'modern Liberals', five of whom crossed the floor, teamed up to defeat freedom of religion.

Anthony Albanese has promised to revisit the issue, making him the third Prime Minister in four years to promise this. But here's why I don't think it will happen. Labor's policy, as enunciated in the latest edition of its National Platform, is to provide taxpayer-funded sex-change operations to 'LGBTIQ young people'.

That is just the tip of the iceberg of Labor's radical LGBTIQ policies. The Greens of course are the same if not more radical on sexual identity politics. The Liberals are facing a post-election-loss identity crisis, having abandoned their conservative base during the Turnbull-Morrison years.

It is doubtful that the Liberals will have the spine to argue for religious schools to be free to hire staff and uphold their religious ethos when it comes to marriage and gender. Look what the 'modern Liberals' did to fairness in women's sports campaigner Katherine Deves during the election campaign. Look at how Scott Morrison, who remains in the Parliament, abandoned Citipointe Christian College at the first sound of grapeshot as its quite reasonable Christian enrolment policy was attacked.

The fourth group of the quad that now dominates the Australian political discourse are the newly-minted teals. They are all left-wing women who hold the same views as Labor and the Greens. The political quad that controls Australian politics is on a unity ticket and will back the political agenda of LGBTIQA+ activists over religious schools any day.

When it comes to freedom of speech, things are also grim. Not even the Abbott Government had the stomach to sustain an argument to remove 18C, the anti-free speech provision of the federal Racial Discrimination Act, which allows legal action to be taken by someone who feels offended. Similar 18C type provisions lace state and federal anti-discrimination laws – just ask Archbishop Porteous. It is under these provisions that I am being sued by two drag queens. Who would have ever thought Australia would come to this?

The Red, Blue, Green and now Teal quad of Australian politics is on a unity ticket. They will not restore free speech and I doubt very much they will legislate any meaningful protection of religious freedom. The game long ago shifted from persevering freedom of speech and freedom of religion to restoring it. Our freedoms were lost in the mail of the Australian Marriage Law Postal Survey in November 2017.

TOOLS OF DEMOCRACY

My lunch all those years ago where Preston Manning, a seminal figure in Canadian politics who almost become Prime Minister, encouraged me to pick up the tools of democracy, put a fresh spring in my step. At the time many Christian leaders were looking for a permission structure to stay out of the same-sex marriage debate as the storm clouds gathered. It was polarising and our opponents had cleverly painted anyone who disagreed as unloving, callous bigots. Who wanted to be seen to be on that side of the debate?

Rather than wade in and publicly de-construct the falsehoods that underpinned every pre-supposition and assertion behind redefining marriage, the majority of leaders wanted out of the public debate. In my view, the silence of leaders was a key reason we lost the 2017 plebiscite. The public only heard one side of the debate.

Today as an organiser for a minor political party seeking to have strong and courageous voices for life, family, faith and freedom elected to our parliaments, the simple idea that I am free and entitled as much as any other citizen to pick up the tools of democracy gives me boldness. There are lots of fine efforts in the culture wars and we need every one of them.

But I am convinced one of the key missing ingredients in the battle for freedom of speech and freedom of religion is a partisan political movement that puts strong and courageous voices into parliament who are willing to sustain the debate for freedom over a long period of time.

We lost our freedoms because principally the Greens did exactly this. They emboldened the left of Labor who won the argument in Labor and then it metastasized to the 'modern Liberals'. The conservative Liberals who believe what you and I do, with a few notable exceptions, are too timid to engage the debate. Even fewer are willing to sustain the debate.

But the Greens are not.

In 2010, Adam Bandt was the first Green ever elected to the House of representatives. In the last sitting week of 2010 he moved a motion in the House of Representatives calling on every MP to survey their electorate about their views on same-sex marriage over the Christmas break. This was a motion, not legislation. It was non-binding. But because Bandt was using the tools of democracy on a controversial issue and one favoured by the press gallery, it got maximum media coverage.

This was just six years after the ACL had helped broker a bi-partisan amendment to the marriage act to put beyond doubt that marriage was a union between one man and one woman voluntarily entered in to for life. Bandt's use of the tools of democracy built pressure for the law to be ultimately changed by 2017.

Do you think Bandt was put off by the fact that when MPs returned in early 2011 and reported overwelmingly that their informal surveys showed the majority did not want same sex marriage? Not at all. He emboldened Labor, speeches continued to be made, multiple private members bills were put up. The use of the tools of democracy was relentless for the next seven years. Do the Liberals have some people like Adam Bandt, willing to fight for the right causes? Indeed they do.

I love the Australian Christian Lobby and gave 10 years of my life to it, starting at a time when paying the wages of a very small staff was a challenge from month to month. The ACL is one of the indispensable organisations we now have in this country and by God's grace, it has serious heft. I'm thrilled to see where it has gone under Martyn Iles' leadership since I left at the beginning of 2018. I spent 10 years walking the halls of Parliament House in Canberra and the State Parliaments around the nation. There were and are many fine parliamentarians who agree with the things you and I do. But sadly, I discovered there were very few willing to sustain debates on the issues that really matter in the culture wars.

The pressure from the party hierarchy in Labor and Liberal to steer clear of these debates is enormous. Senator Claire Chandler from Tasmania has been champion for saving women's sport. But her private Senator's bill was never allowed to be debated, despite a supposedly conservative government holding power in Canberra. In fact, during the election campaign when the heat came from a hostile media, then Prime Minister Scott Morrison said the government had no plans for a bill to save women's sports. George Christiansen's Bill to ensure medical care is rendered to babies born alive after botched abortions – yes it happens and George presented the evidence confirmed by the Parliamentary Library – was not allowed to be debated after it was introduced. It languished on the notice paper and was extinguished with the issuing of the writs for the 2022 election. I doubt it will be resurrected – maybe Senator Alex Antic will do it.

George retired from parliament saying it was just too hard for conservatives, even under a conservative government. Former Liberal Senator Cory Bernardi also left the Liberal party and ultimately the Parliament expressing similar sentiments. But as Churchill said, we should never surrender.

CONCLUSION

Our freedoms are gone and what we have left are under increasing pressure. My friend Bob McCoskrie of the lobby group Family First in New Zealand just had his organisation's charitable status stripped after the Ardern government took action in the Supreme Court. Essentially Family First New Zealand lost its charitable status because the court said arguing that marriage between one man and one woman was not a public benefit. I kid you not. Left wing charities which also engage in political advocacy such as Greenpeace and the Helen Clarke foundation (which fights for legalising marijuana) are able to offer tax rebates to their donors. In the woketopia across the Tasman, George Orwell's dictum that all animals are equal but some are more equal than others applies not to sheep – but to conservative charities engaged in political discourse.

We must not lose our sense of outrage at the double standards and the deployment of not-so-soft power against us. One of the greatest tools we have in a democracy is the capacity to organise ourselves into political parties which can stand people for public office who will fight for our values. This is the missing piece on the battlefield in the fight for freedom in Australia. Let's grab the tools of democracy and build a partisan movement for life, family, freedom and faith before it is too late.

FREEDOM OF SPEECH AND RELIGION: THE CHRISTIAN DIFFERENCE
Alex Sidhu

ABSTRACT

We hear much of 'the right to freedom of speech and freedom of religion' in contemporary western society but what exactly do they mean and how should Christians understand these concepts and their limits? This paper will argue that the understanding of these rights in the Catholic Tradition is not compatible with the dominant liberal understanding, and discuss the implications for Catholic political engagement.

INCREASINGLY WE ARE witnessing governments placing limitations on what individuals can say and do both in public and also in private with regard to biological sex, gender identity and human sexuality, specifically through anti-discrimination law, equality law and so-called 'conversion practices or therapy' laws.[1]

Section 17 (1) of the Tasmanian Anti-discrimination Act 1998 provides for the penalisation of speech or acts considered

1   This term has become ideologically loaded. It is premised on the distorted anthropology which underlies the 'LGBTQI' ideology, which views same sex sexual desire as a 'natural variant' of human sexuality (in other words as a 'good' or 'fulfilling' type of human sexuality, and gender dysphoria as the expression of person's true gender. This anthropology is in conflict with human biological reality and those traditions whose anthropology is premised on human biological reality, such as the Catholic Thomist tradition.

to have caused 'offence' (what one subjectively takes to be 'offensive'). Several prominent individuals have been cited as possibly breeching this section, including Archbishop Julian Porteous and more recently Senator Claire Chandler. The recently passed Victorian Change or Suppression (Conversion) Practices Prohibition Act 2021 seeks to penalise anyone who is in some way perceived to be negative about same sex sexual attraction or sexual intimacy, or attempts to present oneself as the opposite sex due to gender dysphoria. This includes the simple act of praying for someone asking for prayers with regard to unwanted sexual desire or desire to live as if they were the opposite sex.

However the recently published Tasmanian Law Reform Institute (TLRI) final report on 'Sexual Orientation and Gender Identity Conversion Practices', promotes changes to the law which would go far beyond what is contained in these already overbearing, and one might argue illegitimate, laws.[1] Specifically the TLRI report seeks to make statements or practices which promote or defend a so-called heteronormative view of human sexuality, or a binary view of gender based solely on biological sex, a form of hate speech.

We have seemingly reached a point in Western Civilisation (perhaps the first time in recorded human history) where it is becoming illegal or legally punishable to express of defend statements of biological reality or biological fact with regard to human sexuality and sexual difference. We have not quite reached the point where the reading or expression of Christian scripture is illegal, particularly as it concerns statements relating to human sexuality or sex identity, but through the

---

[1] See Section 7.3.3 of the TLRI Final Report on 'Sexual Orientation and Gender Identity Conversion Practices'. https://www.utas.edu.au/__data/assets/pdf_file/0004/1585921/2022.CP.Report32.final.A4_securedwcopy.pdf

various examples in the so called 'same sex marriage' plebiscite and then later in the Israel Folau case it has become clear that it is now commercially acceptable to end employment contracts for merely expressing or acting in accordance with one's Christian faith.[1] If one was cynical, one might believe that the final push to ban at least the expression of particular passages of scripture or the statement of scriptural interpretation on matters of sexuality or gender, is simply being held off until the expression of biological reality is first prohibited. Once this is achieved there will likely be little resistance to prohibiting the publication or expression of Christian scripture.

This move by governments to limit speech and public expression of belief with regard to human sexuality and biological sex, is the result of fierce political lobbying, media and corporate campaigning by activist groups, commonly referred to as 'LGBTQI' over the last 60 years. Governments do no operate in a vacuum as we know, they respond and try and speak to the dominant movements in the culture in order to appear 'relevant'. As the culture has started to change, governments have followed with changes to the law. Since getting legal penalties and restrictions removed for the public expression of same sex sexuality and presenting oneself as the opposite sex in public, this activist movement have moved step by step to achieve legal equivalence between committed heterosexual and homosexual relationships, and between biological sex and gender self-identification. The next stage, (perhaps far from the last stage) is the attempt to get laws instituted that penalise (and therefore silence) those who publicly express an alternative view to the 'LGBTQI' movement on human sex

1   Georgie Burgess, 'Coalition For Marriage anti-ssm event denied by Wrest Point casino, university, campaign claims', ABC, https://www.abc.net.au/news/2017-10-04/acl-anti-ssm-event-loses-venue-after-wrest-point-cancels/9015626

differentiation and sexuality. Hence the recently coined term 'cancel culture', which refers to this effort by activist groups to have any public expression of a view counter to their ideological beliefs 'cancelled' by the media, government, educational and corporate entities and ultimately made illegal. This activism has already been largely successful as it has effectively silenced most who oppose such radical sexuality ideology out of fear of being attacked on social media or targeted in direct action through anti-discrimination or equality tribunals. This has been referred to as the 'chilling effect'.

The response of Christians and others to this 'cancel culture' has been to appeal to the 'right of freedom of speech and freedom of religion' and to seek to get better legal protections for these rights, the latter of which is perhaps the most poorly protected of all the fundamental human rights in Australian law.

But a critical question is how do we best go about this? All attempts to date have seemingly been unsuccessful. In this paper, I do not want to try and provide a detailed analysis of the political efforts that have been undertaken to achieve such legal protections. Rather I want to suggest that in fighting for such protections so conceived we, as Christians, in particularly Catholics, may have inadvertently been undermining what we are actually seeking to proclaim. We have perhaps in the expression of our position adopted language and an approach which is ill suited to the task. Rather than offer a full explanation of our Christian understanding of the importance of religious freedom, we have tended at least in practice to have adopted a kind of liberal approach.[1] We have attempted to use what we believe are 'neutral' terms and arguments lacking any distinc-

---

1   When I refer here to liberalism, I am referring to a tradition of thought in modern political philosophy, whose roots can arguable be found in earlier nominalist thought, but perhaps whose founding contributor was John Locke.

tive Christian context, (something like Rawlsian political liberalism), instead of presenting a full expression of the Christian understanding of what we are claiming in legal protections, which also requires an explanation of our understanding of the nature and role of government. This approach has potentially contributed to an obscuring of authentic Catholic teaching and the full implications of Catholic theological beliefs for the moral and political order.

I believe this argument, and the concerns it raises, share a deep affinity in particular with the work of theologian Stanley Hauerwas on this question, who speaks about the concept of 'freedom of religion' as being a 'subtle temptation' for Christians.[1] Writing back in the early 1990s in the American context where the 'freedom of religion' is a founding ideal for the nation, he observed that 'Christians have been so concerned with supporting the social and legal institutions that sustain religion, we have failed to notice that we are no longer a people who make it interesting for a society to acknowledge our freedom. Put differently, in such a context, believer and nonbeliever alike soon begin to think what matters is not whether our convictions are true but whether they are functional. We thus fail to remember that the question is not whether the church has the freedom to preach the gospel in America, but rather whether the church in America preaches the gospel as true.'[2]

We hear much of 'the right to freedom of speech and freedom of religion' in contemporary western society but what exactly do these rights mean and how should Christians understand them and given the increasing attack on them, and

1 Stanley Hauerwas, *After Christendom*, Abingdon Press, 1991, p 69.
2 Ibid, pp 70-71.

defend what they stand for?

In this first part of the paper I want to argue that a significant problem with contemporary debate about 'freedom of speech and freedom of religion', is a lack of clarity over what we all mean by the concept of 'freedom'. I want to try and show the difference between what I believe is the authentically Catholic understanding and the dominant liberal understanding, recognising that there is a particular temptation on the part of Christians to employ a kind of 'neutralist' liberal philosophical approach in an attempt to appeal to principles and beliefs that the majority of our fellow citizens can understand and might find compelling.

I want to suggest that Christians must resist the liberal approach and indeed more broadly, men and women of good will. I will argue, following the Christian theological tradition, that the concept of freedom only has meaning in relation to the truth. This, for many of us gathered here may sound particularly unexceptional, but unfortunately this is not the case for the vast majority in our society, and this in itself is cause for considerable concern.

It is absolutely critical to understand that one can only genuinely defend 'freedom' or 'liberty' on the basis of a prior commitment to the objective truth. For it is only because of the truth that freedom itself is a possibility, without the truth there could only be the pursuit of desire and feelings and endless manipulation. A reality so dark to even conceive of, it would be far beyond any Hollywood 'horror' movie.

Unless Christians move to return to speaking about freedom and rights fundamentally based in the pursuit of the truth I believe we will ultimately be unsuccessful in getting genuine and lasting protections for the public expression and practice of Christianity, which itself has been essential to the development and major achievements of western civilisation.

But perhaps even more importantly, unless we do this, we will be misrepresenting authentic Christian teaching and impairing the living of the Christian life by believers.

So what is 'freedom', what is a right understanding of freedom?

The concept of freedom is complex and there is no attempt to offer a full discussion here. Rather I want to discuss two particular ways we might understand 'freedom'. First we can understand 'freedom' in terms of having the capacity in our nature for 'choice'. In this sense we can say that what makes human beings different to all other creatures is that they are 'free', they have the capacity for choice, to make decisions, indeed it is a fundamental part of our nature that we have self-awareness, consciousness, and are confronted with choice at every point in our lives.

Unlike animals, who are purely directed by desire and instinct, we have 'freedom', we have to make a conscious decision as to how we are going to act. So in this sense we can say that all human beings are 'free' or have the capacity for choice, or decision making.[1] We might call this the 'anthropological' or existential dimension of freedom, that our nature has the capacity for choosing. But we can use this capacity well or poorly, through the exercise of this capacity we can achieve flourishing of our nature or impede this flourishing.

The second sense of the concept of freedom concerns the situation where outside limitations are placed on our capacity to choose, when we are restricted or prevented from acting in the way we would like. In this context when we speak of 'freedom' we are referring to 'liberation from some kind of

---

1   Freedom in this sense is similar to what Aristotle refers to in terms of the 'rational principle', that what is distinctive about human beings is their capacity for making decisions, in a way that other creatures are unable. See Aristotle The Nicomachean Ethics, Book 1 no 7.

oppression or force which limits us acting as we would like'.

For the Christian then, we can speak of being 'free', or being made with 'freedom', but also seeking 'freedom', specifically freedom from the oppression of original sin. But what we seek as Christians is not a state of perpetual 'freedom', in the sense of endless choice, but one of full human flourishing or eternal blessedness. This can only be attained through Divine grace, but, at least for the Catholic tradition it also requires us to make ourselves into the kind of person we are called to be in Christ, through our actions, through the choices we make. In this second sense of freedom we can speak of at least two types of freedom. Freedom 'from' and freedom 'for'. Isaiah Berlin, the respected philosopher, spoke of these as 'two concepts of liberty', one 'negative' and the other 'positive'.[1]

Typically the most prominent understanding of freedom in our culture has been developed through the liberal philosophical tradition. The core of this conception is the idea that freedom fundamentally involves a 'freedom from' (what Berlin called 'negative liberty') as opposed to a 'freedom for' (what Berlin called 'positive liberty'). This involves an understanding of freedom as an end in itself. Being 'free' involves freedom from interference.

More fundamentally this understanding of freedom is premised on a particular conception of the person, a particular metaphysical anthropology, where the end of human life is simply one of exercising choice. It is not about 'what' you

---

[1] Isaiah Berlin, *Four Essay on Liberty*, Oxford University Press, 1969, pp 118-173. Berlin was suspicious of those who supported a 'positive' conception of liberty and himself was in favour of a form of liberal pluralism, which was more informed by a 'negative' conception of liberty. I am not able to discuss in detail Berlin's substantive position, but I believe his distinction between 'positive' and 'negative' understandings of liberty is important.

chose, but simply that you are in a position to choose. This is perhaps most clearly championed by those described as 'anti-perfectionist' liberals.[1]

I have of course vastly oversimplified the full complexity and nuance of some very sophisticated liberal theories, as developed by theorists such as John Rawls. But what distinguishes a liberal, by definition, is to hold that 'liberty' understood as end in itself, is the most important political principle for human existence, as opposed to human flourishing or one's commitment to God.

The second type of freedom, that of 'freedom for' (or as Berlin would refer to it 'positive liberty'), views freedom as instrumental. Freedom on this understanding is important or necessary in order for individuals to be able to achieve some good, and ultimately the final good, the attainment of which we need for the flourishing of our nature. This conception is premised on a different anthropology to the liberal one, we might refer to this as Eudaimonistic, Aristotelian, teleological or perfectionist, where what matters most is the flourishing of our nature, and that we can only flourish by making the right decisions. Freedom only has meaning in terms of the achievement of human flourishing, knowing and acting according to the truth of human existence, or put differently, to be authentically free is not about simply exercising choice or removing barriers to human choice but rather requires we live our life in a particular way.

On the Christian understanding if the exercise of our capacity for freedom, our decision making, is not directed to the truth, the achievement of our end, then while exercising our

[1] This is the idea that life, or at least politics, should not be about perfecting human nature according to some ideal of the good life. Rather it is about establishing a system of government where all can pursue their own conception of the good life.

freedom we are becoming 'unfree', we are choosing against our flourishing and therefore 'enslaving ourselves in error'. We would be frustrating the nature of our being (as beings made for relationship with God). The state of being 'free' can only be understood in terms of our human nature which is fixed. We will only be 'free' in making those decisions that are consistent with human flourishing. On the Christian understanding, having government not interfere directly with our decisions about how we choose to live our lives is not 'being free', it does not make us 'free'. It simply means we have a type of 'freedom'. This is not an unimportant type of freedom, it recognises the proper limitations of the state. But ironically the historical evidence suggests that Christian faith has tended to be more strongly practiced and lived when believers are being oppressed by government and it tends to wane when 'freedom of belief' is protected.

For the Christian then, being free, understood as having the capacity for choice, and even being free from the interference of others, is not what is most important, rather the exercise of freedom only has worth to the extent that it moves us to flourish according to our human nature. As St Augustine recognised, what point is having a capacity for freedom and exercising that capacity if the choices we make lead us to the loss of heaven and eternal damnation.[1] Through original sin we experience an ontological oppression, an oppression of our 'being' through sin. We will not be free of this oppression without divine grace and ultimately the invitation from God to share the life of the Trinity in Heaven.

The human rights tradition, which has come from the work

1   Saint Pope John Paul II makes this point in his Apostolic Letter on St Augustine, *Augustinum Hipponsensem*, https://www.vatican.va/content/john-paul-ii/en/apost_letters/1986/documents/hf_jp-ii_apl_26081986_augustinum-hipponensem.html

of liberal theorists, champions an understanding of 'freedom' in terms of a negative liberty, a 'freedom from'. They assert simply that human beings by nature have certain rights, primarily a right to self-preservation, and that we enter into society only in order to better protect these 'original' rights. The role of government, on their account, is primarily to protect the 'freedom' of the individual, to structure society so that there might be maximum freedom compatible with at the same time maintaining order. In this approach government is all about individual 'freedom'. The focus is on 'having' rights, not what or how the rights should be used. In this way we can understand the liberal notion of a right to religious freedom as a 'freedom from'. It involves an attempt to 'safeguard' politics from the truth claims of religion, which on Locke's account would cause civil strife if not contained. The effect of this approach is that Christian theological beliefs are restricted from being embodied and lived in the political arena.

Contrary to this, the Catholic tradition while more recently employing the concept of human rights in its social teaching, understands such rights radically differently to the liberal tradition. For the Catholic tradition there are no 'primordial' or 'original' natural rights that inhere in human nature. Rather there is the eternal law, which contains the true ordering of all things, and our way of participating in the eternal law which is either through the divine law or the natural law. The divine law has been revealed through divine revelation as contained in Sacred Scripture, the natural law involves the use of reason reflecting on human experience and observation to reveal the truth. The challenge however in adopting the language of 'human rights' is that most Christians view such rights in a 'liberal' way. The use of the concept of moral rights, such as 'human rights', (as distinct to civil or legal rights, which are different), has, I would contend, negatively impacted how

Catholics understand Catholic moral teaching. Catholics tend to get infatuated with the language of moral rights, and never move beyond this to the core concepts at the heart of Catholic moral teaching (specifically, the truth, fixed nature created by God, human flourishing, and blessedness). Over time they essentially become 'liberals', where the use of the concept of rights is completely detached from truth and human flourishing, eventually driving out authentic Christian faith.

I am arguing for a reorientation in the public expression of Catholic moral teaching as it relates to rights and government, to the ideal of truth. 'Human rights' are not primordial, original or fundamental rather the eternal law is primordial, original and fundamental, and as this concerns the human person what is most important is human flourishing. On the Catholic understanding, the role of government is not fundamentally to protect human freedom, but rather to promote the common good. This promotion of the common good does however involve the recognition of some basic goods which the government is obligated to protect, such as life, marriage etc. There are moral absolutes and government only exercises rightful authority when they respect the moral law and these basic goods, through means such as the enacting of civil rights or protections.

What also seems to have been obscured in Catholic teachings is the proper relationship between the government and rights. The Church's position, properly understood is not that governments are limited by human rights as such, rather they are limited by the eternal law, which we know through the divine moral law and the natural law. Governments have their authority from God alone, and when not recognising God as the source of their authority, either explicitly or implicitly, in terms of their actions they make themselves into a pseudo divinity. If they do not acknowledge the truth, they instead, by implication, make themselves into the source of truth, a false god.

What do we mean when speaking of a right to religious freedom and why is it important?

At the heart of Christianity is a love story, which is only possible by God's respect for human freedom. As already discussed what fundamentally distinguishes humanity from the rest of creation is our 'freedom', the God given capacity for choice. That capacity for choice resulted in our original parents deciding against God in favour of themselves, original sin. But God did not give up on us, instead He sent his only Son, Jesus Christ, to offer himself (a free decision of Jesus) as a sacrifice so that man might be reconciled with God, so that human beings might again be able to enjoy full relationship with God in heaven.

Authentic friendship and love can only exist on the basis of a free and conscious decision. Authentic love cannot be compelled, in involves the free decision to will the good of the other. We can only come to authentically know and love God in freedom.[1] This is why the Church's recognition a 'right to re-

---

1   See the Second Vatican Council document *Gaudium et spes* no 1. 'Only in freedom can man direct himself towards goodness. Our contemporaries make much of this freedom and pursue it eagerly; rightly to be sure. Often however they foster it perversely as a licence for doing whatever pleases them, even if it is evil. For its part, authentic freedom is an exceptional sign of the divine image within man. For god has willed that man remain 'under the control of his own decisions,', so that he can seek his Creator spontaneously, and come freely to utter and blissful perfection through loyalty to Him. Hence man's dignity demands that he act according to a knowing and free choice of what is good, and procures for himself through effective and skilful action, apt helps to that end. Since man's freedom has been damaged by sin, only by the aid of God's grace can he bring such a relationship with God into full flower. Before the judgement seat of God each man must render an account of his own life, whether he has done good or evil.'

ligious freedom' in the twentieth century, properly understood, did not in itself constitute a rupture or break with previous Catholic teaching, some of it particularly hostile to 'rights'.[1] However what these popes like Gregory XVI were condemning in being critical of certain rights, was not the authentic understanding of Christian freedom (freedom for) but the liberal philosophic understanding of such rights, specifically the notion that a right of conscience involved freedom from the truth, that there is a moral right to believe whatever you want.

In recognising a right to religious freedom the Church was not and is not affirming the existence of an abstract right to believe whatever you want, rather it is affirming the reality of human nature as desiring the truth, needing to know the truth, and that a type of 'freedom' is required to come to know the truth. This results in a moral position which holds that individuals cannot be forced to worship or affirm beliefs against their will. This is the original freedom of human beings to decide for or against God. This is a sacred freedom given to human beings, but one with eternal consequences.

As Second Vatican Council document *Dignitatis humanae* makes clear the freedom of religion if it is to be consistent with Catholic teaching must be understood in term of the primordial desire of the human person for the truth. As it states 'men are bound to seek the truth, especially as it concerns God and His Church, and to embrace the truth they come to know, and hold fast to it…the truth cannot impose itself except by virtue of its own truth'. The freedom of religion is presented as a positive freedom, necessary for the person 'to fulfil their duty to worship God' and therefore involves an 'immunity from coercion in civil society'.[2]

1 See Pope Gregory XVI encyclical *Mirari vos*, no 14, https://www.papalencyclicals.net/greg16/g16mirar.htm

2 *Dignitatis humanae* no 1-3. https://www.vatican.va/archive/

For the Christian then the civil or legal protection referred to in terms of 'religious freedom' is more accurately understood as a 'right to know and worship the truth', not a right to believe anything. We, as Christians, support legal protections for religious belief and practice so that people may come to the truth. It is absolutely critical to the integrity of Christian belief that Christians themselves understand this. What I want to suggest is that in order that the Catholic teaching be better understood, the concept of the 'right to religious freedom' needs to be recast in terms of the 'right to pursue, know and worship the truth'. In doing so there can be no confusion that this right can only be a positive freedom.

Further for the Christian it is not that government in itself has the power to grant such legal rights or protections, rather such protections are demanded by the common good. Governments act outside their proper authority when they do not recognise and implement legal protections required by the moral law, as understood through the demands of the common good. What has been missed by Christians, and Catholics in particular, is that the authority exercised by government really comes from God. This belief is not some 'nice symbolic sentiment', it is actually true in the real order things. The state has limited authority which is given by God only for the promotion of the common good. When it does not act within the bounds of this authority it becomes oppressive, and is opposed to human flourishing. It is the role of the Church to call government back into line when it oversteps this authority, as John the Baptist did, it is the role of the bishop to challenge rulers when they step beyond their legitimate authority.

While the actual governments we have are the outcome of

---

hist_councils/ii_vatican_council/documents/vat-ii_decl_19651207_dignitatis-humanae_en.html a complex history of war, power struggles, violence and compromise, nevertheless they are only legitimate and authentic to their nature when they act within the bounds of their God given authority and under the divine and natural law. If they do not respect God's authority, as embodied in this law, they make themselves into a counter divinity, they create a 'new' faith of government as the highest authority.

The Catholic Church does not support legal rights to religious freedom because they are essential to democratic society as such, or because they are required by the principle of human autonomy, choice or freedom, in themselves. These are classically liberal philosophical reasons for supporting the principle of legal protections for religious freedom. We do not support such protections because they are listed in the Universal Declaration of Human Rights, rather this declaration and other international agreements like it only have authority to the extent that they recognise an authentic understanding of such rights.

Indeed all such freedoms, referred to in terms of human rights, only have their foundation in relation to the truth, the pursuit of the truth and human flourishing. Without this they are utterly meaningless, and become mere human assertions. *Gaudium et spes* recognises the difficulties involved in using 'rights' language within a society that is increasingly philosophically liberal, where freedom presupposed to no further good (negative liberty), is viewed as the highest value. It clarifies that 'movements of today by which these rights are everywhere fostered... must be penetrated by the spirit of the Gospel and protected against any kind of false autonomy.'[1] This false autonomy is one that maintains 'that our personal rights are fully

[1] Second Vatican Council, *Gaudium et spes*. No 41, retrieved 10 April 2011, http://www.vatican.va/archive/hist_councils/ii_vatican_council/documents/vat-ii_cons_19651207_gaudium-et-spes_en.html

ensured only when we are exempt from every requirement of divine law'.[1] According to the Church such a conception of autonomy in relation to rights does not maintain 'the dignity of the human person, but [involves] its annihilation'.[2]

We should not understand ourselves as concerned with defending endless choice, or unbounded rights to say whatever we like. We should not understand ourselves as battling for a carve out set of protections in the law to be able to express a dissenting opinion to the prevailing culture, rather we should understand our task as one of seeking to promote and defend the truth of the human person in all its theological richness and beauty, which is required for the possibility of authentic civilisation.

So what does this mean?

In addition to correcting our understanding of the right to religious freedom I believe we must also change the way in which most of us as Christians understand and engage the political order. For Catholics, it is little understood that the Second Vatican Council in the Declaration *Dignitatis humanae*, did not reject the prior, so called 'traditionalist' understanding of the nature of the relationship between faith and politics, which proclaimed and sought to fully embody the social reign of Christ the King, as taught prior to the Second Vatican Council in the writing of popes such as Pius XI in *Quas primas*. Put simply this teaching holds that human society cannot fully flourish without embracing the way of Christ. In other words, without Christ, what is fully human cannot be attained, for it is only through Christ that what is human makes sense and can be fully understood. Or as *Gaudium et spes* puts it 'only in the mystery of the incarnate Word does the mystery of man

[1] *Gaudium et spes*, No 41.
[2] *Gaudium et spes*, No 41.

take on light. For Adam, the first man, was a figure of Him Who was to come, namely Christ the Lord. Christ, the final Adam, by the revelation of the mystery of the Father and His love, fully reveals man to man himself and makes his supreme calling clear.'[1]

This teaching in *Gaudium et spes* is then reaffirmed in *Dignitatis humanae* when it states that the document 'leaves untouched the traditional Catholic doctrine on the moral duty of men and societies to the true religion and toward the one Church of Christ'.[2] Again affirming that the right to religious freedom can only be properly understood as a positive right to truth, a 'right to pursue, know and worship the truth'.

With the Second Vatican Council the Church did not become the champion of a liberal conception of freedom and democracy. It did not put aside the ideal of truth in politics, (which can only be found in Jesus Christ). What it tried to do was to express its traditional teaching on the question of faith and politics in a way that might be better understood by the world. However rather than achieving this end, many have interpreted the documents of the Second Vatican Council, specifically *Dignitatis humanae*, incorrectly, and in doing so unintentionally created more confusion. The exact details of this, I cannot go into here.

The critical point is that if we do not again speak clearly in defence of the existence of an objective truth to human existence, and that it is only in relation to the truth that we can have authentic freedom we will lose the freedoms we so greatly prize as a society. As Pope John Paul II made clear in this encyclical *Centesimus annus*, 'In a world without truth, freedom loses its

1   *Gaudium et spes*, no 22, https://www.vatican.va/archive/hist_councils/ii_vatican_council/documents/vat-ii_const_19651207_gaudium-et-spes_en.html
2   *Dignitatis humanae* no 1.

foundation and people are exposed to the violence of passion and to manipulation, both open and hidden.'[1]

Secondly, unless we correct the dominant cultural understanding of religious freedom as a 'freedom from', instead of being understood correctly as a 'freedom for', we will see dubious organisations take advantage of legal protections they have no right entitlement to. A recent example of this was highlighted by The Australian, back in January of 2021 when the so called 'temple of Satan' was given recognition by the Sunshine Coast University Hospital multi-faith centre as a 'religion' alongside Christianity, Islam and Judaism.[2] However from a Christian perspective, government is not obligated to give special recognition and protection to movements that by their nature are opposed to objective truth, (or more fully put, opposed to truth, beauty and goodness), regardless of whether some refer to them as a 'religion' or not.

Moving from the nebulous expression 'right to religious freedom' to 'a right to pursue, know and worship the truth' would, I believe, help to address this issue. Satanism, by its very nature, is opposed to the truth, this is a clear basis for government to draw the line between what is and what is not acceptable to receive civil protections.

A belief system such as 'Satanism' is not, by its own admission, committed to the good or the true, and therefore cannot be the subject of legal protections afforded to belief systems that do seek what is true and good. The government has a legitimate responsibility in protecting individuals from beliefs that directly attack basic human goods and the very notion of objective truth itself.

1 *Centesimus annus*, no 46.
2 https://www.theaustralian.com.au/commentary/strewth/devil-worshipers-celebrate-important-win-for-religious-freedom/news-story/a549957ff2cfc2ae3a7731be22147ffb

CONCLUSION

The fight to get adequate legal protections for the public expression of religious belief is fundamentally important, indeed, we are also now fighting for adequate legal protections even to express what are basic biological facts about the human person.

However, as I have argued I believe the approach we have been taking has been ultimately undermining our own cause. We will never be able to properly protect the public expression of genuine religious belief, unless we explicitly and publicly speak of such belief in terms of the truth, and insist that government only acts within its rightful authority when it acts as a servant of the truth. It is the loss of a sense and understanding of the objective truth in our culture that, I believe, has led us into this current situation.

We facing nothing less than an all-out fight for the defence of the great achievements of western civilisation. It is time for Christianity to return to a full proclamation and defence of the truth, freed from the distortions of philosophical liberalism.

'CITIZENS OF NO MEAN CITY': WHY CHRISTIANS WILL BE THE PROUDEST AND MOST PASSIONATE DEFENDERS OF OUR DYING CULTURE'S LIBERTIES
David van Gend

IT IS CLEAR from the splendid but sobering papers we have listened to in this colloquium that the better angels of Western Civilisation, like the Elves of Middle Earth, have been 'fighting the long defeat'.

Those who despise our Judeo-Christian heritage now control the high ground of our culture, particularly the fields of education, media, medicine, law and global politics. The task for all of us who love the world that flows from Bethlehem, not Mordor or Beijing, is to stake out and fiercely defend our own cultural space against those who would impose their alien ways.

It's steady work. Since the 1990s, I have played a small supporting role to our faithful pro-life and pro-family organisations as we sought to hammer four defiant stakes into the ground, defining the moral domain that we will not relinquish and where our children's children will still be able to live in liberty, sanity, and relative innocence.

Those four stakes reject the killing of our offspring, the killing of our parents, the desecrating of human life through embryo experimentation, and the trashing of the human trinity of man-woman-child through homosexual 'marriage' and gender ideology.

Around these four stakes we place a boundary rope, a line that shall not be crossed, an assertion of our inalienable liberties of thought, conscience, speech, and association—such as we have exercised so freely today.

For we are proud citizens of a free country, and we claim our birthright. Even an outsider like St Paul had a proper pride as a Roman citizen and upbraided the centurion in Jerusalem for manhandling him.

We, like Paul, are 'citizens of no mean city', even if we have no abiding city; even if the streets of some demoralised Western cities, with their toppled statues and Antifa mobs, are getting meaner by the day.

We, too, will assert our hard-won civic liberty to speak according to conscience, and 'live not by lies'.

Defending this boundary line of core liberties will be difficult; but defend it we will. It is true, as the elven Lord Elrond told Gandalf the Grey, that 'the list of our allies grows thin'. But how invigorating it is to be part of a counter-cultural resistance, a fellowship of free people!

'A day may come', said Aragorn, 'when the courage of men fails, when we flee before the orc-filth of woke atheist culture, but it is not this day! Today we fight, men of the West!'

And so, I have asked three men of the West to help focus our minds on this fight; to give us a one-liner that clarifies a key element of today's colloquium—which has been on the topic of 'Freedom of speech and freedom of religion: the essence of Western Civilisation':

- Mr John Milton will get to the heart of free speech.
- Sir Winston Churchill will define civilisation.
- Professor Christopher Dawson will show the centrality of religion to the culture war that engulfs us.

MILTON

'Give me the liberty to argue freely according to conscience, above all liberties.'

That was John Milton, 400 years ago, appealing to the British Parliament not to enact laws that would prohibit the publication of certain opinions.

Free speech—which means free argument—is the expression of free thought, and the thoughts that matter most to individuals are those formed out of deep conscientious struggle. Without free thought and free argument, we are not free citizens or even free souls; we lose the capacity to defend our deepest convictions and therefore lose the essence of our humanity, which is to live according to what we judge to be true and right.

Free speech—which means free argument—is at the heart of a society that settles its disputes by debate, not guns. It should not be a partisan issue. As the greatest free-speech warrior of the West, Canadian journalist Mark Steyn, has said: 'Free speech is not a left-right thing; it is a free-unfree thing.'

And yet the liberty to argue freely according to conscience is being constricted throughout the Western world in the name of a new and bogus 'right not to be offended'. Steyn speaks from experience: 'In Canada, I committed the crime of 'offending' certain approved identity groups. And there is no defense to that: truth, facts, evidence are all irrelevant. If someone's 'offended', that's that: You're guilty.'[1]

Thanks to Steyn's magnificent push-back against the Canadian 'human rights' establishment, the Canadian Parliament repealed the vilification law under which he was harassed.

In Australia that remains unfinished business, whether with section 18C and the lack of religious freedom legislation at the

---

1 Steyn M., A difference of degree, *National Review*, 2 April 2011, https://www.nationalreview.com/corner/difference-degree-mark-steyn/

federal level, or the 'human rights' tribunals in various States that exist solely to suppress the human rights of free speech and free conscience.

With free speech, it's a matter of use it or lose it—even though standing on your soapbox makes you an easy target. In my case that meant the vandalism of my medical practice by an anarchist painting 'van Gend BIGOT' in red paint across its walls; threats of assault and death during the marriage campaign which the police had to monitor; attempted sabotage, in my view, by the Sydney bosses of a big printing company contracted to print my book against same-sex 'marriage'; an online petition to have me stripped of my medical license because I held unacceptable opinions on marriage.

And this is nothing compared to what friends have put up with, such as Lyle Shelton's office being bombed by a gay activist with an anti-religious grudge when Lyle was head of the Australian Christian Lobby, or others who have lost employment because they publicly supported the No campaign on same-sex 'marriage'. For example, Madeline, a teenager we met at Lyle's and Monica Doumit's marriage campaign headquarters in Canberra. Madeline had posted our slogan, 'It's OK to say no', to Facebook and in response, her employer sacked her. Eight months later, Monica reported in the *Catholic Weekly* that the Fair Work Ombudsman had upheld the right of the employer to sack Madeline![1] That is the cost in today's Australia of expressing a traditional and true viewpoint on a timeless institution.

Beyond vandals, trolls, and corporate bullies we now see 'woke' state agencies doing the bidding of vexatious activists.

1   Doumit M., 'A contract worker sacked for expressing her personal belief? That's scary stuff', *Catholic Weekly*, 15 May 2018, https://www.catholicweekly.com.au/monica-doumit-a-contract-worker-fired-for-expressing-her-personal-belief-thats-scary-stuff/

In my case, this has meant ludicrous cases—eventually thrown out—before the Anti-Discrimination Tribunal of Queensland and the Medical Board of Australia, for publishing mainstream views on marriage and gender that 'offended' LGBT activists.

Against this fake right 'not to be offended', we should affirm that being offended is part of the price of freedom. Hearing things that offend is unavoidable in a society that governs itself by free argument, not by violence. Therefore, fellow citizens, let us take offence in our stride as part of our civic duty—or go live in a nice totalitarian society like China where there is no offence because thought and argument has been crushed into a soulless, offenceless pulp.

The whole question of our core freedoms was meant to be addressed by the 2018 Ruddock Review of Religious Freedom. It was strange to find the head of the Australian Human Rights Commission on the Ruddock Committee, given that the only effective way to protect freedom of speech and religion in an age of vexatious offence-taking would be to defang such Commissions that prowl the boundaries of acceptable beliefs. Professor Rosalind Croucher was courteous when I spoke with the committee, even though I had been blunt in the submission she had before her, where I said:

> *The Australian Human Rights Commission has no mandate to act as the national arbiter of acceptable opinion. For Australian law to adequately protect freedom of conscience and religion, the Human Rights apparatus will have to be relieved of its power to intimidate citizens who express conscientious convictions that are well-founded but out of step with the spirit of the age.*

One thinks of the late great cartoonist, Bill Leak, whose conscience-pricking depiction of the plight of Aboriginal children resulted in relentless and despicable intimidation by our Human Rights Commission.

I also said to the Ruddock committee that their inquiry marks a watershed moment:

> *We can either reaffirm the primacy of the individual conscience, an unusual idea that arose from the unprecedented importance of the individual soul in Christian culture, or we can give primacy to the 'group conscience' of identity politics and sink slowly back into the collectivism characteristic of human history.*

The greatest affirmation of the individual against the collective comes in the *Universal Declaration of Human Rights*, which opens thus: 'All human beings are born free and equal in dignity and rights. They are endowed with reason and conscience and should act towards one another in a spirit of brotherhood.'

Note that the epitome of human dignity is 'reason and conscience', not yet religion. That comes later in Article 18: 'Everyone has the right to freedom of thought, conscience and religion.' This threefold freedom is at the heart of human rights because it is at the heart of human life. These are the freedoms that, throughout history, men and women would die for.

This priority of conscience over religion in a declaration of human rights is important because even agnostics need conscientious freedom. Conscience is the primal faculty of the human soul that perceives right and wrong, the 'aboriginal vicar of Christ' as Saint John Henry Newman put it, and it operates with the same supernatural dignity even in those with no religious worldview.

And so it was a pleasure to see that the Ruddock Review's final report opens with: 'Freedom of thought, conscience and religion is a right enjoyed by all, not just those of faith.'

Faced with that opening statement, a wiser Parliament than the one we have just had would have broadened its proposed legislation beyond a *Religious Discrimination Bill* to include freedom of conscience, whether religious or agnostic, for all of us.

Wiser Parliaments than any we have had, state and federal, would repeal our 'anti-vilification' laws—and these laws would then be found to have been unnecessary as well as unworthy. Where free speech strays into personal attack we already have laws against defamation and, ultimately, against incitement to violence. That is enough.

'Give me the liberty to argue freely according to conscience, above all liberties'—especially where such arguments offend prevailing orthodoxy.

CHURCHILL

Our second great Western man, Sir Winston Churchill, defines civilisation as 'a society based upon the opinion of civilians'. Not based upon the approved and enforced opinion of the elite in their globalist institutions or their social media monopolies or their 'anti-discrimination' tribunals; not upon the rule of the #BLM mob tearing down anything they don't like or can't understand. Civilisation means a society based upon the opinion, the free thought, the free speech, of civilians. Churchill continues:

> *It means that violence, the rule of warriors and despotic chiefs … of riot and tyranny, give place to parliaments where laws are made, and independent courts of justice in which over long periods those laws are maintained. That is Civilization—and in its soil grow continually freedom, comfort, and culture.*

The cultural forces that hate western, and especially British, civilisation, are relentless in undermining its foundations; we have to be relentless in shoring up those foundations. Understanding the sources of our strength may help us to stand firm.

One key source of our strength is our culture's deep institutional foundation in religion. When the future King George V opened the first Commonwealth parliament in 1901, British Australia was already a thousand-year-old Christian monarchy. When my grandparents attended the Queen's coronation in 1953 as representatives of Northern Rhodesia, the oath they heard Queen Elizabeth take was little changed from the coronation oath of King Edgar a thousand years earlier in 973, where he vowed 'to defend the land, uphold its laws, protect its church, and rule justly'.

In turn, Edgar's anointing as king was modelled on the anointing of King Solomon, nearly two thousand years earlier. The only moment at the Queen's coronation that was hidden from the television viewer was the anointing, as that was deemed a sacred moment between the monarch and God; the Queen being the head of the Church of England and 'defender of the faith'.

A culture with a deep foundation in Christian faith will hold a high view of the individual soul and its dignity. As you excavate down into two thousand years of Christian civilisation among the English-speaking people, you find an unwavering conviction that individual liberty must triumph over the tyranny of kings, and that all of us are equal before the law and under God.

And so with Magna Carta, the Great Charter of Liberties of 1215, bad King John and his abuses had to be brought to heel by the Barons at Runnymede. You remember A.A. Milne's poem that starts: 'King John was not a good man—he had his little ways, And sometimes no one spoke to him for days and days and days...' Thanks to this bad monarch, the world got the foundational document upon which 'government of the people, by the people, for the people' would gradually be constructed.

This Anglo-Saxon culture of which we are heirs has been the most successful in creating stable democracy throughout the world and the most resolute in resisting tyranny; a heritage of liberty, in which freedom of speech and freedom of religion came to be honoured more highly than in any other culture at any other time. We are citizens of no mean civilisation.

DAWSON

Christopher Dawson, our third great man of the West, teaches that culture is 'embodied religion', an enfleshment of religion over time; culture is the sum of the ways in which religion becomes embodied in material forms and patterns of life. And Dawson talks about the vital process of enculturation 'by which culture is handed on by the society and acquired by the individual'.

Western civilisation has a crisis of enculturation, or lack of it, in our schools and universities and public life. Our own culture is not being handed on by society—indeed it is being trashed in the minds of the young. But because nature abhors a vacuum, rival cultures are muscling in as the embodiment of alien religions.

The two dominant rival religions at work in our culture are atheist and pantheist -and we should remember C.S. Lewis's warning that it is pantheism, not atheism, that poses the greatest threat to monotheism. That is because atheism, being ultimately nihilistic, can only tear down—the Communists have never built anything of lasting beauty. Pantheism is not nihilistic, and it can build up: it draws its energy from a transcendent mysticism of unity with earth or cosmos, along with the frisson of sexual license that goes with all nature worship, and that is a viable culture-forming religion.

Atheist deculturation
Consider first the atheist wreckers. 'Communism begins where atheism begins', said Marx, and communist animosity to the family was heightened by the perception that family and religion were intertwined in Western culture. After all, the iconic image of Christianity was the mother and child. Marx wrote, 'Therefore after the earthly family is discovered as the secret of the holy family, the former must itself be theoretically and practically destroyed.'[1] The great atheist saw that there is something quasi-sacred about the earthly trinity of father, mother and child, and it had to be destroyed as part of the destruction of religion.

The church was the one relentless enemy of the totalitarians from the days of Marx until the visit of Pope John Paul II to communist Poland in 1979, which tipped the first domino that brought down the Berlin wall a decade later.

But so much damage to religion and family had already been done. From the mid twentieth century, as Paul Kengor documents in his remarkable book, *Takedown*, Freudian-Marxists had realized that fundamental transformation of society would ultimately come not through economic changes but through vast cultural-sexual changes undermining family and married life.[2] Sex could be a devastating instrument if permitted to run rampant, and so they advocated the elimination of

[1] Weikart R., 'Marx, Engels, and the Abolition of the Family,' History of European Ideas 18, no.5 (1994): 664, cited in Kengor, Takedown, see below.

[2] Kengor P., *Takedown: From Communists to Progressives, How the Left Has Sabotaged Family and Marriage* (Washington DC: WND Books, 2015, loc. 1642 Kindle.

141

all sexual restraints along with the destruction of the family, religion, and 'bourgeois' morality.

The final blow was legalising same-sex 'marriage'.

The atheist revolutionaries knew that to deconstruct marriage is to deconstruct the family and destroy the very notion of a natural order. For, as we said endlessly during the marriage debate, if we reject the natural truth of man and woman in marriage, we reject the natural truth of mother and father in parenting, and we ultimately reject the natural reality of male and female itself.

All becomes a genderless, government-defined, nihilistic chaos, which is exactly the objective of the radicals who now control the high ground of our culture.

Pantheist enculturation

Meantime, while the atheists tear down the old culture, the eco-pantheists build up the new culture. They do this by capturing the minds of children, using intense fear and heavy moral authority to compel a child's belief in the coming climate apocalypse.

Over nine wasted years, the Coalition Government failed utterly to expel eco-apocalyptic junk-science from the National Curriculum and so failed to combat the Deep Green terrorising of our children, who now take to the streets weeping over the imminent end of the world and raging against capitalists, meat-eaters and other enemies of the planet.

For these young people, crusading for 'real action to save the planet' gives their lives a serious and even transcendent purpose. It also meets a religious need, providing a form of pantheist spirituality to souls who have long drifted from their monotheistic moorings. Think only of the powerfully pantheist movie, *Avatar*, where the morally pure, deep green creatures on the planet Pandora confront the evil mining barons from central casting who would violate Eywa, the 'All Mother' spirit of the planet.

And now, at Sydney University, you are invited to a conference called 'Nature Feelz', whose organisers say they are 'interested in what it would mean to consider the ecological emotions of beings other than humans'.

Former Climate Commissioner Tim Flannery went the full Gaia in an interview with *The Guardian*: 'we are on the edge of creating a global super-organism' in which the collective human mind will commune with the earth goddess:

> *I think this global super-organism, this global intelligence, will be able to send a single strong and clear signal to the Earth. And what that means, in a sense, is that we will be a regulating intelligence for the planet and we will do what our brain does for our body which is to help create stability, coordination between the parts, and lead to a stronger Gaia, if you want, a stronger earth-system.*[1]

Flannery's 'stronger Gaia' requires global groupthink, 'a global community with a common set of beliefs' sending 'a single strong and clear message to the Earth'. This is a disturbing fantasy, but then all totalitarian systems start off as mere disturbing fantasies.

How much tolerance will there be for freedom of speech and of religion, when those who oppose the cult of Gaia are condemned as enemies of the planet? This fanatical fantasy, this cultural embodying of eco-pantheism, is our very near future. So as we conclude this cheerful end-of-civilisation tale, what hope is there for the good old faith of our fathers?

1   Tim Flannery interview with *The Guardian*, 2011 -excerpts https://youtu.be/SeNDSeknn_c

Our list of allies grows thin indeed, but in any epic adventure there are going to be unexpected and sometimes positive twists in the plot. Consider two groups of fellow travellers appearing from left field whose insights might inject new energy into our ancient religion and therefore into our culture. These are certain agnostic psychologists and agnostic scientists.

Both groups resonate with the deepest idea of our faith: an idea captured in five words of Greek written on parchment in the first century, words which had the power then to create a culture and have power to recreate it now: 'And the Word became flesh'; the Mind of God became man.

First group: the agnostic psychologists

Just this week, a clip of psychologist Jordan Peterson appeared on John Anderson's *Conversations* website.[1] The two men were speaking about the centrality of free speech to Western Civilisation (obviously aware of this impending Colloquium) and Peterson said:

> *The idea of logos in the West is the most sacred concept—if you think about this psychologically, Christ is the ideal of perfection. One of the things the West has settled on is that the perfect individual utters the truthful speech that makes potential into habitable order.*
>
> *That's embedded in the first few sentences in Genesis when God brings the world into being. It's an unbelievably remarkable idea—that individual perfection is to be found in the relationship with spoken truth. That's The Great Idea. Out of that arises the observation that there's nothing more central to the hierarchy of rights than freedom of speech. That's why Christ*

---

[1] John Anderson *Conversations*, with Jordan Peterson on freedom of speech and the logos. 11 July 2022. https://youtu.be/ymcibB-KEdLo

is the word made flesh ... If you want to take the West down, you remove the idea of the Divine Word from the substructure of society.

Conversely, if you want to build the West up, you restore the idea of the Divine Word. Agnostics like Peterson (even though his Jungian psychology is really a benign takeover bid for Christianity) bring the idea of the Divine Logos back to the western mind. Long may his free speech flourish—although I note he has just been cancelled by Twitter.

Second group: the agnostic scientists
Even more exciting is the group of scientists who profess no faith but perceive the Mind of God in the deep rationality of the natural world. Einstein, who saw further into the cosmos than any of us, wrote,

> *'Everyone who is seriously engaged in the pursuit of science becomes convinced that the laws of nature manifest the existence of a spirit vastly superior to that of men, and one in the face of which we with our modest powers must feel humble.'*[1]

He describes how,

> *A conviction, akin to religious feeling, of the rationality or intelligibility of the world lies behind all scientific work of a higher order ... This firm belief, a belief bound up with deep feeling, in a superior mind that reveals itself in the world of experience, represents my conception of God.*

1   Jammer, *Einstein and Religion*, 93.

This lapsed Jew is teaching us once more the fear of the Lord, and that might again be the beginning of wisdom for our culture.

An agnostic Australian scientist, Professor Paul Davies, wrote an entire book called *The Mind of God*, where he explains,

> *Through my scientific work I have come to believe more and more strongly that the physical universe is put together with an ingenuity so astonishing that I cannot accept it merely as a brute fact. There must, it seems to me, be a deeper level of explanation.*

And the late great philosopher Antony Flew, described as 'the world's most notorious atheist', was smitten by the same scientific beauty. In his turn of the century book, *There is a God*, he writes:

> *I now believe that the universe was brought into being by an infinite Intelligence. I believe that this universe's intricate laws manifest what scientists have called the Mind of God. Why do I believe this, given that I expounded and defended atheism for more than a half century? The short answer is this: this is the world picture, as I see it, that has emerged from modern science.*

These reverent agnostics are not far from the first line of the Christian Creed: that we believe in the Mind of God, the almighty creator of heaven and earth, of all things visible and invisible.

If the wider culture were to come back to that Deistic position, how much more interest there would be when we propose the next few lines of the creed, the culture-creating claim that 'for our sake and for our salvation' the Mind of God became flesh and dwelt among us.

I don't know if Antony Flew took that second step before he died, but his unflinching integrity made him say, 'Where do I go from here? … The question of whether the Divine has revealed itself in human history remains a valid topic of discussion. You cannot limit the possibilities of omnipotence.'

On the wall of every science classroom in every Catholic and Christian school should be written the words of the great astronomer Johannes Keppler (who discovered the laws of planetary motion): 'We are simply thinking God's thoughts after him'.

That is the evangelical power of good science and it is cause for hope—but it is far from clear that CathEd would allow such a bold expression of free speech and religious conviction.

Conclusion

Ladies and gentlemen, Christians will remain proud 'citizens of no mean city' and will defend the noblest liberties of our civilisation even as the barbarians reduce it to rubble—because we know that the liberty to speak what is true and love what is good is ours by right, as minds made to resonate with the Mind of God.

But for now, our happy counter-cultural band is in much the same position as the Fellowship of the Ring stuck deep in the mines of Moria surrounded by filthy orcs. Says Frodo to Gandalf, 'I wish none of this had happened'. Says Gandalf, 'So do all who live to see such times, but that is not for them to decide. All we have to decide is what to do with the time that is given to us. There are other forces at work in this world, Frodo, besides that of evil … And that is an encouraging thought.'

SHEPHERDING WOLVES TO SAVE OUR FREEDOMS
Veronika Winkels

ABSTRACT

From the public intolerance and exclusion of Margaret Court to the Secular Inquisition of Cardinal Pell, a culture that can't live by its own values, can be played to advantage. The role of Christians is to hold leaders, governments, and the wider cultural landscape to their new post-Christian values, even if these are at variance with their own. The balance between bringing the Divine Logos into the world by speaking true Christian virtues; and employing a language that can be recognized and understood by all in a society that grows more distant and unfamiliar with its Christian roots is the challenge for today's Christian. Her world must be kept distinct from the secular one, yet at the same time, seek the common ground in culture. This has been tried before, yet the result is often a dilution (and therefore distortion) of the Christian message, costing its respect by Christians and non-Christians alike, because it avoids risking anything. In contrast, when the values of secularism are exposed as lacking integrity, potency and richness, compared to the Christian worldview, they are weakened. It is in this climate that religious freedoms are less threatened; and Christians, having preserved their distinct identity and worldview, possess something Christians and non-Christians alike will consider worthy of respect, and protection.

INTRODUCTION

THE REASON I am here, speaking about freedom of speech and religion in Australia, and joining in a conversation about what can be done to protect these incredible gifts of our heritage, is because of a news article I read eighteen months ago. I was nursing my nine week-old daughter, my fourth child, and scrolling the news on my phone, (a terrible habit at the best of times).

I landed on an article that related a discussion then underway in British Parliament. A minister was proposing changes to terminology in the realm of women and motherhood. Notably, that the terms 'breast-feeding' should be changed to 'chest-feeding,' to be more inclusive of transgender people.[1] Likewise, we should talk about pregnant 'people' not pregnant 'women,' to the same end. Of course, as a freelance journalist, I had been keeping abreast (or I should say, 'a-chest') of similar developments occurring across the Western world over the years, but this one was a last straw moment. I was literally nursing my baby while reading, so the proposed legislation felt like a personal attack. I was worse than offended, I was irate. The process was from that moment to founding a new magazine, which I named Mathilde (meaning 'battle maiden') happened with amazing speed. I voiced my idea to a few friends, and since then, formed a team of Orthodox Christians, Catholics and one self-described 'Christian atheist.' All believed in a publication that would advocate for 'reclaimed feminism' and for 'seeking truth, not political narrative'; that would promote virtue as opposed to virtue signalling, and resilience above victimhood.

Since we published our first issue in November last year, we have received incredible support and encouragement. We interviewed tennis legend Margaret Court for our first issue[2], and discussed the hypocrisy of progressives who would not tolerate her religious freedom to believe in the traditional definition of marriage. She has since then been subjected to vitriol

1   Hayley Dixon, 'Midwives advised to use terms such as "chest-feeding" to be gender-inclusive,' *The Telegraph*, 09 February 2021

2   'Keeping Politics Off Court', *Mathilde*, Issue 1, 2021

and exclusion, public shaming and slander. There have even been calls to change the name of the Melbourne arena which is named after her. Last year, the fiftieth anniversary of her first grand slam went largely unrecognised. Her views, it would seem, diverged from the kinds of 'diversity' that have been deemed acceptable by the powers that be.

Political cartoonist and national living treasure Michael Leunig, came on board for our second issue, to discuss losing his job at The Age for a cartoon depicting the COVID vaccine mandate in a critical light.[1] Speaking to these public figures, and many others since founding Mathilde has made me realise how very real are the threats to and abuses against freedom of speech and religion in our country. I present, therefore, what I believe to be the key to recognising and saving these freedoms; not alone as *Christiani contra mundum* — against the world, but in some instances, in union with those who do not even subscribe to religious belief, but who understand why protecting these freedoms are critical for democracy.

WORDS MATTER

'In the beginning was the word and the word was with God, and the word was God.' This opening line of St John's gospel teaches us just how significant language is. Sometimes millennia in the making, words carry meaning, and carry layers of meaning, according to how they have been employed in the past. The more we familiarise ourselves with the different contexts a word has inhabited, and to what effect, predominantly through reading the great Western Canon, the richer in meaning and potency that word becomes, in any new context. Take for example the word 'love.'

---

[1] 'Cancelled: Interview With Michael Leunig', *Mathilde*, Issue 2, 2022

One of the most beautiful early Christian declarations of love can be found in the First Letter of St John. He writes, 'Beloved, let us love one another; for love is of God, and he who loves is born of God and knows God. He who does not love does not know God; for God is love' (1 John 4:7-8).

It has become more acceptable now to say that, 'love is love' than 'God is love.' But the tautology, the circuitous 'love is love', gives the impression of saying something, of having meaning, when in fact it says nothing, means nothing. Shakespeare's 'Love is not love which alters when alteration it finds,'[1] sounds similarly circular, but its depth of meaning and poetry is qualified by a simple word 'which'. The Bard meditates on the 'if/then' which the impoverished mantra 'love is love' does not.

Language and meaning is rich territory upon which Christians can really expose the poverty of the secular worldview that currently dominates our Australian culture and society, and they can cause a bit of mischief doing so too. We can test the sincerity of secular sentiments of love and declare, 'we love God…and, apparently, 'love is love'.

WORDS ARE FREEDOM

Wittgenstein said, 'all I know is all I have words for.' Speech is, in a very real sense, itself freedom. When I interviewed world-renowned ethicist Margaret Somerville,[2] she related how once after giving a talk, a woman approached her and said, 'thank you. I feel like I already believed everything you said today, but I didn't have the words to say it.' Retelling this story, Margaret broke down in tears, and she said, 'that's all I want to do—give people the words to say what they believe.'

1 William Shakespeare, *Sonnet 116*
2 'Things On Which We Can Agree: Finding A Common Language With Margaret Somerville', *Mathilde*, Issue 3, 2022

She related how younger generations have been equipped with a woke vocabulary, which can be so incredibly impregnable to outsiders. This is because only a select 'elite' has full mastery of the politically correct nomenclature, and this because they themselves are its architects.[1] The double tragedy of this is that the new woke vocabulary also cuts off its young purveyors from accessing the vast treasures of the past. To repeat the phrase: 'all I know is all I have words for.' The world that is being articulated for younger generations is one that fails them so much, denies them so much. It sets up false dichotomies and cuts them off from the hard-won wisdom and knowledge, and the inspired poetry of the ages. This wisdom has become virtually inaccessible to younger generations saturated in woke language, because its concepts can only be comprehended beyond the self-reliant woke vision of reality. There is nothing morally neutral about employing the kind of language that does such things.

It's a vision that is innately xenophobic—hostile and derogatory to outsiders, and harbours a special abhorrence for tradition which is, in the words of G. K. Chesterton, the 'democracy of the dead'.

WORDS HAVE BEEN WEAPONISED

St Francis of Assisi said, 'always preach the gospel. When necessary, use words.' Witness is a powerful thing. But in a society that now freely flaunts its disdain of the 'permanent things', in the words of T. S. Eliot, it is growing increasingly more urgent to 'use words.'

When the media, corporations, governments and leaders bring out their buzzwords of inclusivity, diversity, tolerance

---

[1] 'Modern Times: Interview with Camille Paglia & Jordan B Perterson,' *Youtube*, retrieved 25 August 2022

and such, what they are really doing is pulling out their trump cards, knowing full well they are engaging in a language that has been tacitly accepted as irrefutable. It's a cheap move. And any Christian who does not wish to be one day accused of quietism, is bound to hold to account leaders, governments and the wider cultural landscape to their self-prescribed progressive standard of values, even when these are at variance with their own. Clarifications need to be demanded. Terms qualified, contextualized, critiqued. The example of Margaret Court and the Secular Inquisition of Cardinal Pell as another, breach the neo-cardinal virtues of tolerance, 'being nice', inclusivity, and diversity. Yet this vocabulary is the very instrument by which the hypocrisy of those who live and breathe it can be most effectively exposed.

Roger Scruton writes in his introduction to Dietrich von Hildebrand's memoir, My Battle Against Hitler, that:

> *The relevance of von Hildebrand's story has by no means diminished. Extremist ideologies are again growing around us, and we hesitate to describe them in their own language, for fear of provoking them to pursue their aims. Reading von Hildebrand reminds us that there is only one sure remedy against an ideology of hate, and that is to expose it to public criticism and to affirm what it denies. The ardent faith that inspired von Hildebrand is not easily recovered in our sceptical times. But through his love of truth and his brave opposition to a public culture of deception, he bore witness to values that we still share.*[1]

---

1 Dietrich von Hildebrand, *My Battle Against Hitler: Defiance in the Shadow of the Third Reich*, Ed. Trans. John Henry Crosby, Intro. Roger Scruton, New York: Crown Publishing Group, 2016.

RECLAIMING FREEDOM

WORDS WE CAN SHARE

Towards the end of defending the freedoms we have been discussing, a further art we need to practice, is to strike a balance between bringing the Divine Logos into the world, refusing to compromise Christian values; and employing a language that can be recognised and understood by all in a society that grows more distant and unfamiliar with its Christian roots. Our Australian societies and governments are turning more and more to the postmodernist reduction of every aspect of life to what is already known. It is not only uncomfortable and unfamiliar with mystery and uncertainty, but also hostile to it, because by their nature, these things cannot be controlled. I discussed this too with Margaret Somerville. As she observed, postmodernism, stripped back to its fundamental aim, can be summed up in that one word 'control'. Control over our own lives and over others. This is how she understands the pro-euthanasia advocates she is daily engaging in debate with. I agree that this need for control is the secular solution for abating the fear of the unknown, and of suffering. And it either reduces itself to nihilism in the understanding that the cause for control is futile, or in Secular Humanism, which places Man at the pinnacle of existence, and therefore the arbiter of morality, not God. Postmodernism, as a way of life, pales in comparison to the richness and gloriousness of the Christian life. We see this precisely through its vocabulary.

Karl Marx said, 'keep people from their history and they are easily controlled.'[1] If we have no knowledge, understanding or appreciation of the past, we have no roots, and having no roots, we become drifters. We're told this is a virtue — of openness — but the age of pandemic proved how this lack

---

1   *Letters of Karl Marx and Friedrich Engels 1842-1895*, Trans. Donna Torr International Publishers, 1968.

of rootedness made us infinitely compliant. Which is why I deliberately chose 'openness' as our theme for Issue 2. In order to explore what it really means, and when it becomes its own kind of prison.

The purpose of being open, I think, is to 'test everything' as St Paul exhorts us to. But the directive follows on, as you know, to say 'hold fast to what is good' — Mathilde's motto. As part of that, an idea I think Christians need to explore more, is that 'he that is not against us is for us,' (Mark 9:40).

Another article relevant to this discussion which we published in Issue 1 of Mathilde one called 'The Conservative Greenie.'[1] It sought to expose how many progressives exploit the environment cause as a front for other political agendas. But that was not our only intention. We also wanted to highlight the common cause of the environment to all people, iterating the link between conservatism and conservation. By reconceptualising the issues of our day, or rediscovering the origins of the words used to discuss them, we hope to find we actually have more common ground upon which to engage with secular culture than we realise, and which we are not currently harnessing.

In contrast, when Christians engage in the public sphere with euphemisms, abstractions and platitudes that are so often used by politicians and bureaucrats to hide behind and avoid controversy, they lose a huge opportunity to attract the respect of people of goodwill and integrity. The result is always a dilution of the Gospel message, to make it more 'palatable', and accommodating of secular lifestyles. But this effort results only in losing the respect of Christians and non-Christians alike, because it avoids risking making enemies. And it's a false peace.

1   Natasha Marsh, 'The Conservative Greenie,' *Mathilde*, Issue 1, 2021.

MAKING MISCHIEF

Archbishop Julian Porteous believes that 'the notion of discrimination needs to be rescued... and restored as a positive virtue to be sought and prized.'[1] What we now call having a 'good bullshit detector' is no less than the virtue of what we used to call a discriminating mind. This includes the ability to see through the fog of jargon, nebulous statements and obfuscations and perceive right from wrong, truth from lies and integrity from expediency. Words which serve the sincere pursuit of truth and wisdom, need their reputations restored if we are to extend the limit of our world.

By choosing words that cut through abstractions and get to the heart of a matter, Christians show they mean serious business. And it earns respect from the secular spectator. Inversely, by choosing words that are easily recognised, such as 'tolerance,' 'diversity,' and 'community,' not in echo of the innocuous and disingenuous sentiment they usually carry, but in a way that calls them out, and the hypocrisy with which they are so often yielded, is not only a good thing, but also devilishly fun to do. It's always an added satisfaction to beat someone at their own game. In this way, Christians prove they can show charity, but that does not mean they suffer fools gladly. They ought not to.

An example of someone Christians can imitate in this is British comedian Russell Brand. He's outrageous, but he genuinely doesn't care what anyone thinks, and is happy to point and shout that the emperor isn't wearing any clothes. He has a gift of turning woke language on its head, and has amassed a social media following in the millions for it.

When engaging with a faceless organisation, partisan media or an individual who is manifestly seeking power, and not the

---

1   Arch. Julian Porteous, 'The Virtue of Discrimination,' *The Record*, 14 March, 2011

betterment of society; making mischief is perhaps one of the surest ways forward to rebuilding our freedoms. 'The worst thing you can do to the devil is laugh at him', St Thomas More is said to have quipped.

When engaging, however, with people who do not seek cheap seats on the moral high ground, and are not opportunistically seeking the nearest Christian as a way to it, I think Christians ought to take a more amenable attitude. Honesty and intentionality with words is a major force that many non-religious do better than those who profess faith. These are the people who are curious, who desire the truth, who follow the evidence wherever it may lead, and are willing to step into that space between groups where real conversation happens. And it happens. University of Melbourne professor, Holly Lawford-Smith, spoke with me about feminism and the trans narrative.[1] This woman is not, I believe, a Christian. She is a self-proclaimed radical feminist, and stands for many things I don't. But she has shown honour and integrity recently in launching a website[2] which calls for testimonies from women about sharing women-only spaces with transwomen. Nowhere does she state on the website any hostile views towards transgenderism. She is simply collecting stories from which she can garner knowledge and understanding. That is in fact her job, at least ostensibly. But the backlash she received simply for creating this forum has all but cost her career, her professional reputation and opportunities for advancement in her career. Sitting down with her on Melbourne University grounds, in a beer garden, she was aware of people staring at us. This was not a paranoid woman. If anything, she was temperamentally as phlegmatic as they come. But our conversation was not

1   'No Conflict They Said,' *Mathilde*, Issue 2, 2022
2   noconflicttheysaid.org

approved. She had betrayed the narrative of Identity Politics, which is watertight insofar as mainstream academia is concerned, by suggesting that adopting trans unquestioningly might, in fact, harm women. She is still feeling the penalty of her initiative, which is doing great work to hold the trans narrative to account. She's someone to admire and imitate in the virtues of commitment to truth, and courage, no matter what the cost.

The beauty of the Christian worldview is that it accepts it has something to learn from everyone, and so can in good faith learn from such people. To use a modern term, Christianity has always had an inherent 'growth mindset.' It believes, as St Edith Stein said, 'those who are seeking truth, are seeking Christ, whether they know it or not', and so, working at its best, is open to the wisdom that has been gained from outside its tradition. Aquinas owed so much of the development of his thought to Aristotle; and without the ancient philosopher's influence, we would not have the Summa, a monolith of Christian literature. Today, many Christians admire the work of Jordan B. Peterson, Douglas Murray and others who do not call themselves Christians. In so far as we esteem these figures, we encourage unity with others who share respect for them.

More and more I understand how far humility can get a person in life. I can believe I am closer to the truth than my secular neighbour, but that doesn't exempt me from making the effort of trying to see why they may believe me wrong, and they right. We could keep butting heads, as pride would have us. I've seen this in some Christian circles, those who fall for the trap of building themselves up by knocking down 'the other side'. We fall for the sin of stereotyping just as much as we get stereotyped. We think we know who we're dealing with, but more often then not, I think we underestimate the goodwill, and authenticity, and basic goodness of many, perhaps most, of the people whose views depart, even sometimes radically, from our own. I'll err on the side of hope.

ALWAYS DARKEST BEFORE THE DAWN

Add to this, that I believe we are culminating towards a historical moment, where more individuals are beginning to believe what George Orwell said—that 'Progress and reaction have both turned out to be swindles.'[1]

Christians often take the position of being in the dock, of being the one on trial. And unfortunately, though understandably, this has created a subculture, amongst serious Christians, of defensiveness and even suspicion. But if I am right in believing that we are progressing to a stage where secularism is revealing itself more and more for what it is — something that comes up short in answering the deep human need for the infinite mysteries of truth, beauty and goodness — this should give Christians the confidence to turn the burden of proof back on their secular counterparts, and speak about their traditions and values not from a posture of apology, but conviction. The idea that life is made meaningful by shouldering the heaviest burden one can carry, as popularised by Jordan B. Peterson, has generated huge interest and support. This clinical psychologist (which is perhaps as close as one can get to secular priesthood) reveals, more than perhaps any other contemporary thinker today, how starved people are for meaning, young people especially. And more, they are growing ever more painfully aware of it, arguably in direct proportion to the distance and disparity

---

1 Sonia Orwell and Ian Angus (eds) *The Collected Essays, Journalism, and Letters of George Orwell, 1920-1940*, Secker & Warburg: London, 1968, the full quote is: 'Progress and reaction have both turned out to be swindles. Seemingly, there is nothing left but quietism — robbing reality of its terrors by simply submitting to it.'

between their paradigm of well-meaning but ultimately vacuous tenets, such as 'love is love', and the one that proclaims instead that 'God is love.'

Christians should revive their confidence that individuals yearn to be challenged, not accommodated. When the values of secularism are exposed as lacking integrity, potency and richness, as unable to present individuals with a higher calling than to 'be nice,' they are weakened; in philosophy, and in example, whenever those who make the utterance fall short themselves.

I'd like to end with the words of Margaret Somerville again. I'm not sure if she was intentionally echoing Scripture when she said, 'you don't actually need a lot of ethical people in order to save a culture or society.' But it reminded me of how God promised Abraham he would not destroy the city for the sake of ten just men (Gen. 18:32). If Australia can muster up just enough just people, willing to lose favour in the cause for freedom, by embracing our roots and calling upon the wisdom of the ages; by engaging in Christian apologetics unapologetically, by seeking the common ground between all people of goodwill, and by building fresh connections between ideas that have been ossified in the bland and bastardized language of progressive politics; freedom of speech and freedom of religion have a fighting chance.

And Christians, having preserved their distinct identity and infinitely richer and hope-filled worldview, will possess something both Christians and non-Christians alike will consider worthy of respect, and protection.

OUR CONTRIBUTORS

Kenneth 'Difff' Crowther is a consultant working in education and operational strategy. He worked in secondary education for thirteen years, teaching Literature, Philosophy and Media, and holding positions including Head of Secondary and Head of Liberal Arts Implementation. He now splits his time between working with schools focussed on classical liberal education, being the Head of Operations at a technology start-up company, and undertaking his PhD. He holds two masters degrees with a research interest in Early Modern literature and culture, and lives on a small off-grid farm with his wife and four young daughters. In whatever time he has left he hosts three podcasts: 'Educating Humans', about classical education; 'The Pursuit of Love', a business, psychology and philosophy podcast; and 'Chiron', a podcast about the history of bad ideas and how they've shaped our world today.

Dr David Collits graduated from Sydney University with a Bachelor of Arts, majoring in history, and a Bachelor of Laws, for which he was awarded first-class honours. He completed a Master of Arts (Theological Studies) (With High Distinction) and was awarded a doctorate in theology in 2021 from the University of Notre Dame, Australia. His thesis explored the hope and history debate in fundamental theology, exploring the cleavages between the *Communio* and *Concilium* schools of contemporary theology. David is currently Lecturer, Catholic Theology in the School of Philosophy and Theology at the Sydney Campus of the University of Notre Dame. He has previously worked on the personal staff of Archbishop Anthony Fisher OP and Justice Macfarlan of the New South

Wales Court of Appeal, and as a lawyer. In 2015, he won The Archbishop of Sydney Prize for Excellence in Postgraduate Theology. He resides in the Blue Mountains, west of Sydney, with his wife and five young children.

Dr Kevin Donnelly AM is a Senior Fellow at the Australian Catholic University's PM Glynn Institute and one of Australia's leading conservative authors and commentators. He is a strong advocate for Christianity in the public square and the importance of religious faith in what is an increasingly secular age. Kevin writes regularly for the print and digital media, including The Australian and the Daily Telegraph. Kevin also appears regularly on Sky News and is the editor of *Cancel Culture and the Left's Long March* and *Christianity Matters In These Troubled Times*. Kevin taught for 18 years in Victorian government and non-government secondary schools, has benchmarked school curriculum in an international context and in 2014 he co-chaired the Commonwealth Government's review of the Australian national curriculum. In 2016 Kevin was made a Member of the Order of Australia for services to education.

Monica Doumit is the Director of Public Affairs and Engagement for the Catholic Archdiocese of Sydney, engaging in policy and communications for issues such as abortion, euthanasia, marriage and religious freedom. She was also the communications director and spokeswoman for the Coalition for Marriage during the 2017 plebiscite on marriage. She is an adjunct senior lecturer in law at the University of Notre Dame Australia and a regular columnist for the Catholic Weekly. Prior to working for the Archdiocese, Monica spent ten years working as a corporate lawyer in Sydney and London, and holds degrees in law, medical science, finance and bioethics.

Lucas McLennan is Senior History Teacher at a Catholic secondary school in Melbourne. He writes: 'I completed an Honours Degree in History and my teaching qualifications at Monash University. I recently completed a Master of Education from the University of Melbourne. I completed my thesis on the Education policy of the first Anglican Bishop in Australia, William Grant Broughton. My earlier Honours thesis examined Australia's compulsory military training schemes between Federation and the First World War. I have a strong interest in Australia's political, religious, and cultural history. Outside of my work, I serve as the Edmund Burke's Club of Australia's president, where we regularly hold talks on various aspects of political history and philosophy. I have also published articles in *News Weekly*.'

Archbishop Julian Porteous was born in Sydney and was ordained a priest for the Archdiocese of Sydney on September 7, 1974. He served as an assistant priest in the parishes of Kingsgrove, Manly, The Entrance, Woy Woy and Mona Vale and in 1999 was appointed parish priest of Dulwich Hill. He has always been actively involved in evangelisation, particularly among young people, and was instrumental in establishing the Pastoral Training School (now known as the Summer School of Evangelisation) which, since 1984, has formed thousands of young Catholics in their Catholic faith and in the pastoral skills necessary to contribute to the Church's evangelising ministry. In January 2002 he was appointed Rector of the Seminary of the Good Shepherd in Sydney.

In 2003 he was named Auxiliary Bishop of Sydney by Pope St John Paul. He has been a strong advocate of the New Evangelisation called for by Pope St John Paul II. Archbishop Julian established an Office for Evangelisation, CREDO, which has been responsible for a number of important evangelisation initiatives, including CRADIO, a digital radio service which promotes the New Evangelisation.

Archbishop Julian was installed as Archbishop of Hobart on 17 September, 2013.

Lyle Shelton is National Director of the recently re-birthed Family First political party. His previous work history includes serving the Australian Christian Lobby for 10 years, five as managing director. For more than 20 years he has been a keen participant in Australia's culture wars first as an elected member of the Toowoomba City Council through to his present involvement in minor party politics. During the 2017 same-sex marriage plebiscite he was a director and spokesperson for the Coalition for Marriage. Lyle has written for The Australian, The Courier Mail, The ABC online, The Spectator online and has been a regular media commentator, appearing on Sky News, the ABC's Q&A, Channel 7's Sunrise, ABC News Breakfast and Channel 10's The Project. Lyle's book, I Kid You Not – Notes from 20 years in the trenches of the culture wars has sold 3400 copies. Lyle has a Bachelor of Arts in journalism and was a former Group Commodities Editor for Rural Press Limited. He lives in Sydney with his wife Wendy. They have four adult children and one grandchild.

Alex Sidhu is the Private Secretary to Archbishop Julian Porteous. He has degrees in Arts (Hons) and Commerce from the University of Melbourne, as well as a MA in political theory. He has completed an MPhil in Theology (Christian Ethics) at the University of Oxford and is currently preparing to submit his Doctoral Thesis at Oxford on the change in Catholic Social Teaching that took place from the late nineteenth century in relation to democracy and human rights. Alex has taught at the University of Melbourne, in the Department of

Politics, and was a sessional lecturer at the John Paul II Institute for Studies on Marriage and Family in Melbourne, before its closure. He is currently a sessional lecturer at The Lachlan Macquarie Institute.

Veronika Winkels is Founding Editor of *Mathilde*, a journal for 'holding fast to what is good', exploring culture, women, and the legacy of Western tradition. She has degrees from The University of Melbourne and The University of Divinity in History, Philosophy and Theology. She lives in Melbourne with her husband, Tristan, and their four young children.

Dr David van Gend is a family doctor and frequent contributor to national debates on bioethics. He lives in Toowoomba, Queensland, with his wife Jane and three teenage sons. He was born in Zambia, central Africa, into a pioneer family of missionary doctors and farmers going back to Robert Moffat and David Livingstone, and in his early years lived in seven Commonwealth countries – mostly in New Zealand – before studying medicine at the University of Queensland.

Since 1994 David has been Queensland secretary for the *World Federation of Doctors who Respect Human Life*, an international association of doctors defending the traditional Western medical ethic. Since 1996 he has been a spokesman for TRUST, an association of doctors, lawyers and prominent citizens opposing euthanasia but promoting palliative care. Since 2002 he has been national director of *Australians for Ethical Stem Cell Research*, which opposes embryo destruction and cloning.

Since 2010 he has been a spokesman for the Family Council of Queensland on same-sex marriage and surrogacy, and since 2011, President of the Australian Marriage Forum. David has debated bioethical issues on national television programmes such as ABC Lateline, The 7.30 Report, and SBS Insight, and has published dozens of articles in major Australian newspapers and journals.

David has testified on seven occasions before Senate Committees – against human cloning and embryo experimentation, against the abortion drug RU486, in defence of pro-life pregnancy support services, against euthanasia and homosexual marriage. He has given parliamentary briefings in five States and federally on a range of subjects, and in May 2006 he spoke to the United States Senate Values Action Team on stem cell research and cloning.

www.ingramcontent.com/pod-product-compliance
Lightning Source LLC
Chambersburg PA
CBHW050314010526
44107CB00055B/2239